# FRIEDLÆNDER
# FROM VAN EYCK TO BRUEGEL

## VOLUME TWO

MAX J. FRIEDLÆNDER

# FROM VAN EYCK
# TO BRUEGEL

EDITED AND ANNOTATED

BY F. GROSSMANN

VOLUME TWO

THE SIXTEENTH CENTURY

PHAIDON

ALL RIGHTS RESERVED BY PHAIDON PRESS LTD
5 CROMWELL PLACE · LONDON SW7

FIRST PUBLISHED 1956
SECOND EDITION 1965
THIRD EDITION 1969

PHAIDON PUBLISHERS INC · NEW YORK
DISTRIBUTORS IN THE UNITED STATES: FREDERICK A. PRAEGER · INC
III FOURTH AVENUE · NEW YORK · N.Y. 10003
LIBRARY OF CONGRESS CATALOG CARD NUMBER: 69-19803

Translated from the German
by Marguerite Kay

Cased (in one volume)
SBN 7148 1375 3
Paperback (in two volumes)
SBN 7148 1377 X (Volume 1)
SBN 7148 1378 8 (Volume 2)

MADE IN GREAT BRITAIN
TEXT PRINTED BY HAZELL WATSON & VINEY LTD · AYLESBURY
COLOUR PLATES PRINTED BY HUNT BARNARD & CO. LTD · AYLESBURY
MONOCHROME PLATES PRINTED BY CAVENDISH PRESS LTD · LEICESTER

# CONTENTS

*VOLUME ONE*

Foreword vii

Introduction ix

The Geography of Netherlandish Art 1

Jan van Eyck 6

Petrus Christus 14

Rogier van der Weyden 16

Dieric Bouts 26

Hugo van der Goes 32

Hans Memlinc 41

Gerard David 48

Geertgen tot Sint Jans 53

Jerome Bosch 56

Plates

Acknowledgements · List of Plates · Index of Places

*VOLUME TWO*

General Remarks on the Sixteenth Century 65

Quentin Massys 70

Joachim de Patenier 78

Joos van Cleve 87

Jan Provost 93

Jan Gossaert 97

Jan Joest 107

Jan Mostaert 113

Lucas van Leyden 121

Jan van Scorel 128

Pieter Bruegel 135

Plates

Acknowledgements · List of Plates · Index of Places

# NOTE

Friedländer's *Von Eyck bis Bruegel* was first published in German in 1916 and a second, enlarged edition appeared in 1921.

The first English edition was published by the Phaidon Press in 1956, in the author's ninetieth year. It contained over three hundred illustrations, and was reprinted with corrections in 1964. This third English edition is issued in paperback as well as in cloth. The paperback edition has been divided into two self-contained volumes, the first covering the fifteenth century and the second covering the sixteenth century.

# FROM VAN EYCK TO BRUEGEL

## THE SIXTEENTH CENTURY

# GENERAL REMARKS ON THE

# SIXTEENTH CENTURY

HISTORIANS of art like to present the turn of the century as an Epoch and begin a new chapter even when describing Northern painting. The familiar contrast 'Quattrocento' and 'Cinquecento' in the South tempts us to make a similar incision in the North. The historian's passion for classification and superstitious belief in the mystery of numbers play their part in converting what was in fact a gradual transformation into a sudden change, whereby impartial observation becomes coloured.

Nevertheless it is permissible to emphasize some features as characteristic for the sixteenth as opposed to the fifteenth century—provided we remember that these traits emerged at intervals, here and there, and over a period extending well beyond and before 1500.

Not a single painter of the sixteenth century combined all the features of the new age in his work. We can enumerate the symptoms but are forced to admit that, of all artists who represent the sixteenth century for us, it is only by one or other aspect of his work that the individual one is stamped as a child of his age. Almost all the painters who began to work between 1490 and 1510 are in some way firmly rooted in tradition, a fact that is overlooked by historians who, whether from ignorance or in the interests of clarity, simplify the historical process. In certain fundamental points Quentin Massys is more archaic than Hugo van der Goes. And an account that places the Louvain master at the beginning of the new period but is forced to include the Ghent master in the old period falsifies the observed facts.

The creative power of Netherlandish art decreases considerably during the second half of the fifteenth century as can be seen particularly at Bruges. Apart from Hugo van der Goes and Geertgen we search in vain for courage and enterprise. Neither Memlinc's pleasant exploitation of inherited wealth nor the passive late-flowering art of David contain seeds for a new beginning.

The period around 1500 offers a confused picture in which simultaneous but widely diverging efforts can be observed in plenty. The character and general conditions can best be defined in negative terms.

Art at the beginning of the sixteenth century lacks confidence and assurance, is without roots and outside the law. Aim and content are no longer determined by the tradition of craftsmanship and ideas; a vacuum has arisen into which comes a wide and varied influx. Even in the past, art historians noted the appearance of Italian forms as an outwardly striking symptom and interpreted it as the real cause of a far-reaching change. The most naive theory, though admittedly hardly to be found in recent literature, presupposed everywhere a 'visit to Italy'; which in each case lured the artist away from the national Netherlandish manner and brought him into the orbit of Italian art.

Rogier visited Italy in 1450 but there is no evident effect of the foreign climate on his formal language. A century later Pieter Bruegel travelled through Italy without perceiving anything of Italian art. If Jan Gossaert or Scorel were transformed in Italy—for good or ill—this denotes exhaustion, lack of resistance, an inner void. The inability to keep up their end is by no means confined to the—greatly overestimated—relationship with Italy. We need only recall Dürer's effect on the Netherlands, first when his engravings and woodcuts arrived singly and then, in 1520, when he himself came and disseminated his prints in such profusion. The German artist was certainly not valued as a painter superior in every respect, he was probably even sharply criticized, but his inventions and richness of composition were seized upon and his prints extensively copied. Hunger reigned and nourishment had to be taken wherever it could be found.

Even in the heroic age of Netherlandish art, even in the first half of the fifteenth century, invention did not flow freely. The predominant role of Rogier van der Weyden can be explained by this general weakness. The strength of Netherlandish art lay more in the searching penetration to the details than in the general conception of the whole. In the sixteenth century it was on invention that a perverted ambition was concentrated. Desire and talent were fatally divided.

A long list of characteristics could be formulated for the new age, but even a tolerably complete survey of personalities and monuments evokes the uneasy feeling that the exceptions constitute a dangerous threat to the rules and that all generalizations are nothing more than half-truths. Nevertheless, in my opinion the sum-total of half-truths does to some extent give an accurate overall pattern of the extraordinary medley of Netherlandish aims in the period between 1490 and 1520.

In the fifteenth century the painter worked modestly, in the spirit of the craftsman, but the artist of genius by his very nature—though not as his aim—produced personal and individual achievements. In the sixteenth century the manners of genius were aped by all. The small masters, who in the fifteenth century worked unassumingly according to the rules, became wild and undisciplined and strove for some bogus originality by exaggeration and ostentation. The craftsmanship began to disintegrate, for on the one hand careful and accurate methods were despised by the vainglorious artistry of the individual and on the other the instinct of gain favoured a more standardized and commercially profitable production with slipshod workmanship and mechanical repetition. On the technical side there was appreciable deterioration. But it was not until the period between 1530 and 1550 that the worst results of this decline were revealed. The general public now made greater claim than ever before and demanded what was new and fashionable rapidly and at little cost. The increasing export of art works to Spain, Germany, Sweden and Denmark, especially from Antwerp, brought the final depression in the quality of painting.

In place of the quiet, firmly defined form preference was now given to agitated, angular forms. The illusion of movement was sought in many small ways and turbulence produced by eccentric attitudes, violent distortions and postures. Incapable of giving new form to the old themes from within, the younger generation was usually content to rake and pile up the old with new trimmings and in a new guise.

Absorbed in the religious content, the artist's one aim and purport had been to evoke it in all simplicity, but this attitude was now replaced by a cold arty ambition (Jan Gossaert) or by an easy charm of manner (Joos van Cleve), by personal sentimentality (Quentin Massys) or by a delighted interest in accessories and stimuli, which were supplied in continually increasing doses (the 'Antwerp Mannerists'). Naturalness, the striking illusion for its own sake—not to serve a purpose—was now sought. The indifference to the content, which was re-interpreted, turned upside down, borders on the frivolous. Once art begins to lose its bearings, to interrupt the organic growth from native roots, to seek chance contacts rather than inner relationships, to be guided by ambitious aims rather than deep-seated impulses, stylistic changes proceed at a hitherto unknown pace. Nervous discontent compels a talented artist like Lucas van

Leyden to mirror the entire confusion of the age in his personal development, and this, moreover, within a particularly brief span of life.

Architecture and décor seem to offer a suitable criterion for an objective assessment of the contrast between the fifteenth and sixteenth centuries. Almost exactly at the turn of the century the Netherlands pass from national Gothic to Italian Renaissance. But even here the process, on closer consideration, appears fairly complex. To begin with, the Gothic style was not abandoned but disintegrated, became unrestrained and degenerate. Not only Italian or would-be Italian Renaissance forms replaced the Gothic ones but also half understood Romanesque motifs— such as the chevrons in early paintings by Orley. The desire to emphasize the remoteness of biblical and legendary scenes, to show off historical knowledge and at the same time to add the spice of the exotic to the representation, was responsible not only for the choice of Italian forms, which were regarded as antique ones, but also for arbitrary inventions.

The delight in decoration runs riot, unhesitatingly mingles Gothic with apparent Renaissance. We rarely find any understanding of architectonic form, of proportions or functional qualities. Knowledge of the Italian Renaissance was derived from doubtful sources and the unassimilated elements were plastered on anywhere. The changing taste in architecture and decoration must in no way be taken seriously. The generally uninformed and superficial use of Italian motifs does not reveal a stylistic ideal that could be regarded, as some writers have done, as the essential driving power.

Almost all the characteristics that I have set out here as signs of disintegration could equally well be interpreted as the stirrings of a new creative spirit. The longing for a great, free art emancipated from the Church can be traced almost everywhere by optimistic seekers. Even in the perfunctoriness of the technical treatment, in the broader, more comprehensive, coarser execution it is possible, bearing in mind the distant aims of seventeenth-century art, to discern a beginning as well as an end. The thick oily painting of an Engelbrechtsen, the broad and fluent brushwork of Jan van Scorel, can be considered as promising seeds on Dutch soil. And the moment forceful talents appeared they were able to push forward successfully down paths that had seemed to lead astray as, above all, Pieter Bruegel.

The new age, which tore down barriers everywhere, offered a wider horizon, richer possibilities, knowledge and incentives, temptation and opportunity, poison and nourishment. The dangers were more fatal for the minor than for the medium talents, for the latter could find some protection against mannerist affectation in the direct and careful observation of nature. It took time for the Netherlandish sense of reality to find its bearings in the enlarged field, for the new possibilities to be exploited, for the new demands to be satisfied, and for the stimuli from the South to be assimilated. The critical transition period lasted almost a century.

# QUENTIN MASSYS

QUENTIN MASSYS was born in 1466 and died in 1530, which makes him a generation younger than Hans Memlinc, a generation older than Bernaert van Orley. What we know of his work was done in full maturity and in old age. We can follow his work without coming upon serious gaps from about 1506 until almost 1530 and can discern the direction that he took. Everything prior to 1506 is obscure or only dimly illumined by hypotheses. It is of little consequence whether the master was born in Antwerp or, as now seems more probable, at Louvain. Even if we were certain that he had spent his youth and apprenticeship at Louvain and had absorbed nothing but Louvain art during his formative years it would not throw much light on his art. We know a little more about Louvain art around 1480 than about the contemporary art in Antwerp—but it is still precious little. The threads that have been spun from Dieric Bouts, the chief master at Louvain, who died in 1476, to Massys are tenuous indeed. Aelbert Bouts, Dieric's son, seems to have been head of a productive workshop at Louvain around 1480 and we think we can recognize the products. But we must not exclude the possibility that artists unknown today made a deeper impression on the young Massys than did the meagre Bouts tradition that we do know.

The only practicable way is to begin where the master's art is fully and richly developed.

By a fortunate coincidence the two accredited works, outstanding apart from their size, are dated or at least can be dated. These two works differ from one another in subject-matter; the sudden change of theme brought astounding variety and richness.

167–168      The altarpiece of *St. Anne* from Louvain, which is now in the Brussels gallery, is inscribed with the date: 1509;[1] the altarpiece with the *Lamenta-*
166 *tion over Christ* at Antwerp was set up in 1511. By making the plausible assumptions that Massys did not work simultaneously on both altarpieces, that the date 1509 marks the conclusion of work on the Brussels altarpiece and, finally, that a period of two years each is not excessive for completing the two sets of five large paintings, on these assumptions

---

[1] Commissioned for the chapel of the Confraternity of St. Anne in the church of St. Peter's at Louvain in 1507, cf. Friedländer. *Die Altniederländische Malerei*, VII, 1929, p. 114.

we are entitled to regard the two works as fruits of the well-spent years 1508–1511. In 1508 Massys was 42 years old; he had been master at Antwerp since 1491, and had probably won fame and recognition for considerable achievements, so that great things were expected from him.

Much as we should like to be able to recognize the line of development by a comparison of the two works, there is little hope, in view of the small time interval and the widely differing subject-matter, of drawing reliable conclusions from such a comparison, particularly as the two altarpieces are not equally well preserved. The contrast, at first sight so striking, is due in part at least to the fact that whereas the Antwerp altarpiece is in perfect condition the Brussels one, as a result of vigorous 'cleaning', has lost much of its colour values and plastic quality.

The central panel of the Brussels altarpiece is tapestry-like with a  167 surprising absense of spatial illusion and centralized lighting. It is tempting to assume that for his large-scale compositions Massys turned to tapestry designers, who were the real representatives of monumental surface decoration in the Netherlands, that if he were accustomed to smaller-sized panels he would be driven to follow the tapestry composi-tions. At any rate, his *Holy Kindred* painting would make a masterly design for a wall-hanging. It is very possible that Massys did make designs for tapestries and that this type of work played a part in determining his style. One thing is certain: around 1500 in the Netherlands very few artists indeed were as qualified as he was to undertake such commissions. Much of his personal manner is reflected in the tapestries—and moreover in the finest ones—that have survived from about 1500.

The figures in the central panel of the *St. Anne* altarpiece in Brussels are of equal size, of equal compositional importance, have a community of feeling and are like in spirit. Since they are all of the same kin, this almost monotonous lack of contrast is well-suited to the subject. On the wings, where the dramatic incidents would permit a diversity in the emotional content, the general flavour remains unchanged. As opposed to the archaism and rigidity of the composition, the expressive quality, inspired throughout from the central creative impulse, has a sentimental appeal. A sensitivity that is almost too sweet, an elegance that tends to affection, certainly seems less appropriate for this virile and daring century than does the emphatic subjectivity with which these emotions are stamped.

The human beings with their spiritual sensibility, more feminine than masculine in character, of ladylike reserve, who shun vulgarity and coarseness, seem charged with the tension of a subdued grief. Intent on preserving the stillness of the place, on maintaining their own dignity, they appear reserved with lightly parted lips and downcast eyes. Bodies, heads and hands are permeated by a restrained pathos. A repressed, not fully clear language echoes across to us, more like a song the words of which we do not understand but which from its melody suggests depths and thoughtfulness. The delicate creatures with their fine hands do not proclaim their inner excitement obtrusively and seem like half-transparent vessels which are for ever challenging us to guess at the contents. Admittedly, once we have examined Massys' entire production the secret loses something of its attraction in that the refined and sensitive spirituality appears everywhere, regardless of subject-matter—almost a mannerism. Massys somehow reminds one of a preacher who by force of habit adopts the pathos of his sermon for everyday language.

Almost prudishly modest, Massys drapes feet and ears, and loves to depict his holy children fully clothed. The human beings show signs of over-breeding with a slightly degenerate charm. The holy figures are fashioned with a conscious sense of beauty; no 'character heads' will be found in the *Holy Kindred*. Irregular or caricature-like forms as well as portrait features are reserved for the antagonists and executioners and for the mob, who are distinct from the ruling caste. Evil is represented as ugliness, all too clear, almost naked, painfully accurate, neatly and smoothly executed with deformations, disfigurements and distortions.

The costume is discreetly adapted to the refined humanity, an attire that does not in the least correspond to the dress worn in 1508 in the Netherlands. The desire to transport figures and actions away from the present by giving them exotic pieces of costume, in particular orientalizing headdresses, played some part, but the master's taste and his love of large areas of selected local colours, of flowing, as it were melodious, drapery folds played a still greater part in producing a freer interpretation of the cut of the garments. The simple guilelessness of the older artists is replaced by a suspicious attitude to nature. Working selectively and guided by a definite taste in what he accepts and what he rejects, Massys strives consciously towards the ideal, towards a refinement of vulgar reality by emphasis and contrast.

In the softer light and in the greater spaciousness of the cathedral the
166 Antwerp altarpiece must formerly have made a less irritating impression than it does today in the museum. It takes time to collect ourselves after the deep but not flawless impression. The tragedy of the Passion is expressed less movingly as a whole than in the individual heads and hands. In the even light of day the predominant impression is that of the

VI. Quentin Massys: *Portrait of a Canon*. Vaduz, Liechtenstein Collection

iridescent splendour of the broad areas of local colour. The symmetry of the almost inflexible groups contrasts distressingly with the realism of each detail. And the smooth silky glaze of the painting seems unsuitable for the large size. The eye searches in vain for an organization of parts to suit the dimensions, for strong contrasts of light and shade, for dominant accents.

We hesitate to trust our first impression and sense something of the chill breath of artistry in the consciously primitive archaic manner.

The ten chief figures, approximately equal in size, are all arranged, not without difficulty, at equal distances from the spectator, so that all the heads are of equal importance as if set by a stage manager who does not wish to offend any of the actors. The whole width is densely packed so that the middle ground is completely covered—eliminated. Everywhere the eye, which longs for a depth to correspond to the height and the width, comes up against the hedge of figures that tower over two-thirds of the picture. There is no connection and no transition from the figures to the landscape background, which is added to fill the free strip at the top. In the painting of the background with its multiple small parts no attention is paid to the proportions of the whole. The immense distance between the grounds is not expressed, at least not by pictorial means. Massys composes like a tapestry designer and paints like a miniaturist. In spite of the harrowing conflict resulting from the master's critical position at the threshold of two ages, the indefatigable care and sensitivity with which the forms are worked in detail over the wide surfaces arouses our astonishment and admiration.

In the two great altarpieces the personality of their author is expressed so eloquently and in such unforgettable accents that we cannot doubt, despite all possibilities of change, that we have grasped the immutable core of his art and can proceed with confidence to assemble the other surviving works by his hand. It may well be that not until fairly late, when he was at the height of his fame, did Massys dare to express his subjectivity clearly and with assurance, so that earlier works—and what an enthralling task it would be to trace them—will show his characteristic traits less clearly and we must be prepared to recognize in bud what we already know in maturity.

In the Brussels gallery are two *Madonnas*, one enthroned, a full-length 164 figure, the other in half-length, both of which were claimed decades ago by Ludwig Scheibler as works, comparatively early ones, by Massys. With full justification as I believe. The panels are heavy and warm in colour, filled with deep melancholy. The small Madonna, the one in half-length, is arresting with her broad face dominated by dark wide-open eyes. What reminds us of Massys in the first place is the smooth surface, the subtle modelling which with superb skill gives a gentle swelling roundness to the bodies. The Children in both pictures resemble one another and their dull secretive air and the expression of helpless sadness in their eyes, familar in the eyes of animals, recurs in work of the maturer Massys style. The undulating drapery in the larger *Madonna* confirms the attribution to Massys.

These two *Madonnas* are a little earlier than the altarpiece of *St. Anne*, how much earlier it is difficult to say. To these can be added the *St. Christopher* in the Antwerp gallery; in the general effect it, too, is dark and is a little reminiscent of Dieric Bouts in the intensive blue and red patches. Though, it is true, the darkness could in this case be explained by the evening light.

W. Cohen's endeavour to trace the derivation of Quentin's art[1] is based on erroneous presuppositions. In the first place, the *Head of the Saviour* in the Antwerp gallery, which to Cohen's mind represents the connecting link between Massys and the Louvain studio of Dieric Bouts, is most certainly not a work by our master but only a particularly successful work by Aelbert Bouts and therefore does not come into consideration. Next we must reject all the conclusions that Cohen so cleverly drew from the Valladolid altarpiece. With a certainty that is unusual for him, C. Justi claimed the Spanish wings for Massys. But as I myself do not accept Massys' authorship I can ignore Cohen's conclusions of a Dutch influence.

Of Quentin's portraits, the one of a *Canon* belonging to Prince Liechtenstein is, as far as I know, generally accepted. The portrait of Aegidius at Longford Castle (probably done in 1517[2]) has been more frequently mentioned than studied. Its authenticity cannot be questioned. Whether its pendant, the second half of the diptych, the portrait of Erasmus of Rotterdam, survives in the Roman version (in the Corsiniana,[3] formerly G. Stroganoff Collection) I cannot venture to decide. The master's most mature portrait, probably also his last, is the one at Frankfurt which, after some extrordinary misconceptions, is now firmly and generally established. The man seems to address us with the air of a rhetorician or actor.

VI
179

178

172

---

[1] *Studien zu Quinten Metsys*, Bonn, 1904.

*[2] The date 1517 is now established from the correspondence of Sir Thomas More, for whom Aegidius and Erasmus had their portraits painted by Massys.

*[3] In *Die Altniederländische Malerei*, VII, 1929, pp. 41 ff. discussing the portrait again, Friedländer expresses no doubt about the authenticity of this version.

In his passion for innovation the intelligent artist seeks to find a pictorial theme that embraces figure, movement, hands and head, and wishes to depict the individual in an action that is characteristic for him. The pictorial theme is not always clear but the interest is always directed to the intellectual qualities which strive to express themselves, and a spiritual relationship is deliberately established between the spectator and the person represented.

The *Portrait of a Man* at Northwick Park[1] is similar in composition to 173 the one belonging to Prince Liechtenstein. The indifference with which that excellent work is regarded is also shown to two more modest portraits, a man and a woman in the Oldenburg gallery. To this group I am adding 174–175 a relatively archaic *Portrait of a Man* in the Chicago Art Institute and one 176 of a younger man belonging to Lord Amherst (*Arundel Club*, 1909 No. 7, 'German School').[2] Who is represented in Lord Amherst's portrait? 'Portrait of Gonsalvo da Cordova' we read in the publication. The motto written in beautiful Roman lettering FIDELITER ET EXPEDITE, the singular huntsman's costume with the sleeves that appear to have been slashed with a sword, and the unusual moustache give an urgency to the problem of who the man can be. The supple posture, the elegant hand, the lightly parted lips, the look of suffering, the desire to speak, seem characteristic for Massys.

The best way to grasp the distinctiveness of Massys' pointed character studies is to compare them with portraits by Holbein, in which the healthy objectivity and inner calm seem classical next to the romantically insistent subjectivity and excitable pathos of the Antwerp master.

A few pictures with approximately life-sized figures, such as the half-length painting of *Christ* and its pendant, the *Mater Dolorosa*, in Antwerp (the corresponding panels in London are probably copies), or the half-length figure of *Mary Magdalen* in the same museum, the *Money Changer* 169, 177 in the Louvre (dated 1519?),[3] the *Madonna*, formerly Rattier Collection, now Louvre (dated 1529), a many-figured *Ecce Homo* privately owned in 170 Madrid,[4] and several other works by the master, take their place alongside the large altarpieces and confirm the impression they made, without enlarging the overall picture.

I feel it incumbent to put in a word for some small-sized paintings. Massys' art changes with the changing dimensions. In a new guise, seen from a new side, its nature is revealed anew and completes and supple-

*[1] Now in the National Gallery of Scotland, Edinburgh.
*[2] Present whereabouts unknown.
*[3] By Friedländer and other authorities the date inscribed on the painting is now read as '1514'.
*[4] Now in the Prado, Madrid.

ments our notion of it. The need to speak of the small pictures is the more urgent because they have been either overlooked or falsely judged, and not one is of any consequence for the popular idea of his art.

If the master's execution does not always appear to accord with the monumentality for which he strove, an easily achieved harmony can at least be expected in works of modest dimensions. And in fact small panels do exist of immaculate polish in which the supple drawing, the exquisitely sensitive movements vibrate in perfect unison with no trace of discord, and in which the remoteness from nature, the spatial structure and the arbitrary independence of the local colouring from natural lighting seem far less questionable or archaic than in the large pictures. One such small-figured work is the altarpiece with four panels in the Munich Pinakothek from which the over-painting has been removed and which has been successfully restored to its original condition. From the Boisserée collection some of the parts had passed to Nuremberg, others had been exhibited in the Pinakothek—the *Virgin on the Crescent*, the *Trinity*, *St. Sebastian* and *St. Roch*. To these may be added the two small panels with *St. John the Evangelist* and *St. Agnes* from the von Carstanjen Collection, at present in the Pinakothek.[1]

171

The *Standing Madonna* in the Lyons museum,[2] so frequently misunderstood, belongs to this group, also the *Madonna* in half-length formerly in the Aynard Collection.

The decision is more complicated in respect of a group of Passion scenes, some of which are of lesser quality and must be regarded as workshop productions. The group is self-contained and consists of a *Crucifixion* belonging to Prince Liechtenstein,[3] a *Crucifixion* in the National Gallery, London, a third very weak one in the Brussels gallery, two triptychs in the Harrach Gallery, Vienna, and the Musée Mayer van den Bergh, Antwerp. Further a *Lamentation over Christ* in the Louvre and finally the nude kneeling figures of female penitents in the Johnson Collection, Philadelphia, and a fragmentary *St. John the Evangelist* in the Padua museum.

Everything produced by Massys testifies to wide culture and conscious striving for refinement, testifies also to a personal taste that shrinks from the coarse and the common but seeks out the rare and the exquisite. The master would fain go beyond his native land to satisfy his aristocratic needs. If he absorbed anything of Southern art it was certainly Leonardo

*[1] Now in the Wallraf-Richartz Museum, Cologne.
*[2] A better version of this composition has come to light later. It is now in the collection of Count Antoine Seilern, London.
*[3] Now in the National Gallery of Canada, Ottawa.

da Vinci whom he felt as a kindred spirit. Perhaps he was familiar with pictures and drawings by Leonardo and schooled his own drawing and modelling on that great example. In one instance at least we can pin down a concrete relationship between the two masters. In the Poznan Museum, there is a large *Virgin* from the Raczynski Collection the inconsistency of which intrigues the critics. The Virgin in full-length is seated out-of-doors turning to one side, the Child is playing with the lamb. Leonardo's celebrated *Virgin and Child with St. Anne* is the model for the composition, but instead of sitting in St. Anne's lap the Virgin Mary is seated on high ground. Massys need not have known the picture that is now in the Louvre; perhaps he used a cartoon, a drawing or a copy of it (many such still exist today). In any case the relationship is instructive.

The picture from the Raczynski Collection has a competent and carefully detailed landscape, which looks purely Netherlandish, and comes up abruptly against the figure. The landscape does not seem to be by the same hand as the figures. The understandable idea has been expressed that it is by Patenier—but I do not find the attribution convincing.[1]

A—certainly inadequate—knowledge of the teachings and achievements of Leonardo seems to have informed Quentin's endeavours and to have supported his tendency to look for higher ideals away from home. It seems to us that in the elaborate complexity of movement, in the suppleness of the bodies and in the subtlety of the modelling we can perceive an ideal inspired by Leonardo.

*[1] In *Die Altniederländische Malerei*, VII, 1929, p. 48, Friedländer regards the attribution of the landscape to Patenier more favourably.

# JOACHIM DE PATENIER

IN van Mander's scanty account of Joachim de Patenier we find two statements that seem to be erroneous. The place of his birth is given as Dinant. But Guicciardini, who is more reliable, calls the painter 'Giovacchino di Pattenier di Bouines'. Whereas van Mander gives Bouvignes as the birthplace of Herri met de Bles, Guicciardini speaks of 'Henrico da Dinant'. Bouvignes and Dinant lie close together on opposite banks of the river Meuse.

According to van Mander, Patenier entered the Antwerp guild in 1535—which is incorrect. The correct date is 1515. The wrong date is not due to a slip of the pen. In his first edition van Mander wrote quite correctly 1515 but in the list of errata altered it to 1535 and repeated 1535 in his second edition. In 1535 a Patenier was in fact entered as master in the Antwerp guild, namely a Herri Patenier.

These strangely fluctuating dates encourage us to accept the hypothesis that Herri met de Bles is identical with Herri Patenier. On the one hand we find Joachim's birthplace confused with that of Herri met de Bles, on the other hand the date that is correct for Herri Patenier is applied to Joachim. Some person who could not distinguish between the two painters named Patenier may have supplied van Mander with the wrong date and perhaps at the same time given the wrong place. The deduction assumes some importance for Herri met de Bles, who, if he really was called Patenier, may have been a relation (perhaps a nephew— 186 Joachim does not seem to have had sons) of the older artist. Failing other dates it would be important to establish that Herri became master in Antwerp in 1535. In the engraved portrait the 'painter with the owl' looks about fifty. Judging by the costume the portrait can hardly have been done before 1560. So that Herri does not seem to have been born before 1510 and in 1535 would not have been older than twenty-five.

As regards Joachim, the question: Dinant or Bouvignes is of no consequence.

This master died in 1524. In 1521 Dürer made a silver-point drawing of him. Patenier's portrait engraved by Cort is obviously based on Dürer's drawing. The painter looks about forty-five. If he was born in

1475, Joachim, when he came to Antwerp in 1515, would have been about forty and prior to that must have worked elsewhere.

The three signed paintings by Patenier that are known to us (Karlsruhe, Antwerp, Vienna) have similar inscriptions: *opus Joachim D. Patinir* 184, 185 (Patinier).[1] The genuineness of the inscriptions is beyond doubt. A *Landscape with the Holy Family*, signed and dated 1520 (?) has recently appeared on the London art market. The Vienna panel with *The Baptism of Christ* seems to offer a good starting-point.

Patenier was a landscape painter, perhaps the first Netherlander to regard himself, and to be regarded, as a landscape painter, like Albrecht Altdorfer in Germany. Therein lies his fame. Dürer, who was on friendly terms with him, calls him the 'gut Landschaftsmaler' (the good landscape painter). How highly the specialist was valued is made abundantly clear by the fact that two of his greatest contemporaries, Quentin Massys and Joos van Cleve, collaborated with him: they painted the figures and he added the landscape.

At Middelburg, so van Mander writes in his vita of Joos, there was in the possession of Melchior Wijntgis a very beautiful *Madonna* by Joos for which Joachim Patenier painted a very beautiful landscape.

C. Justi made the pertinent observation that in the *Temptation of St. Anthony* in the Prado the landscape is by Patenier but the figures by 180 Quentin Massys. Van Mander's remark and the observation in Madrid force us, or at least permit us, to reckon with the possibility of such a collaboration also in other cases. We must in future beware of overlooking the possibility that the figures in Patenier's pictures were painted by other hands.

Landscape painting as an independent subject was late in appearing. We can regard on the one hand the painter's desire to depict and on the other hand the public's desire to see as mutually beneficial and inspiring factors. It was not sufficient for a painter to conceive the idea of painting a landscape and to be capable of doing so, someone also had to be there who was ready and willing to buy the picture. In our day natural landscape, whatever portion of it, from whatever corner of the world, whatever the season or time of day, is so unhesitatingly accepted as a fully valid and adequate pictorial subject that we find it difficult to conceive of conditions in which this was not the case.

Around 1520, in Patenier's day, conditions—conditions of a transition period—were roughly as follows: Netherlandish artists liked painting

---

[1] In addition two paintings by Patenier in the Prado are signed: *St. Jerome in a Landscape* and the *Temptation of St. Anthony*, even though in the latter case the figures are by Quentin Massys.

landscape and in their compositions gave increasing space, scope and importance to landscape. The public shared this liking. When people bought a *Holy Family*, a *St. Jerome* or some such edifying work they were delighted with the bit of landscape that was thrown in.

Though reduced to mere accessories, the figures were responsible not only for the title but also supplied the theme and the starting-point for the composition.

Patenier spins out the narrative in a leisurely way. The sequence in time that cannot be shown in one picture is smuggled in as a juxtaposition of scenes. The wider spacing of the episodes—possible because the land-scape could be extended in depth and width and the structure varied whilst the figures could be made tiny and concealed—makes the juxta-position seem less unnatural, less primitive than, for example, in Mem-linc's panels with the *Passion of Christ* or the *Joys of the Virgin*, though in principle they were similarly composed.

The landscape, though predominant, does not form the content of the picture but only the setting.

Geographical and topographical interests, if not geographical historical knowledge, mingled with a genuine love of nature which, as yet only budding, unconscious of itself, put forward no definite claims but found incidental satisfaction.

The remoteness and strangeness of the events was expressed in the extraordinary and surprising aspect of the landscape. The more sensa-tionally the surroundings differed from the familiar flatness the more natural and suitable they became as the background for sacred adventure.

The district of Dinant, the master's home, is rich in picturesque rock formations. Without doubt the impressions and the study of the surround-ings promoted his understanding of the formation and texture of rock. But it would be wrong and unhistorical to believe that Patenier produced nothing but images of his native scenery. What he absorbed served only as material, as a means of expression, and it was the tendencies just indicated that determined the fashioning of this material.

The desire to build a deep stage on which many things could be enacted and to offer interesting sights to the eager sightseers resulted in mountain views and distant prospects. Patenier surveys the land from the mountain peaks. The naive delight in the sheer quantity of the area surveyed, and therefore dominated, and the thrill of excitement at the monstrous shapes of nature, sensations that have survived today in the most banal of touristic pleasures, had their share in determining the beginnings of landscape art.

The painter's skill in conjuring miles of the countryside onto the small picture panel was admired. The interest in geography, stimulated by the great discoveries of the age, added to the delight in this convenient opportunity of getting to know foreign parts.

Patenier's geographical descriptions would have been sadly restricted had he kept to the laws of scientific perspective construction. Without the least hesitation he constructed his landscape from more than one point of view. One point of view was not sufficient for the whole as well as for the parts. All the horizontals, such as ground surfaces, water surface, paths are seen from above and the horizon is correspondingly high. On the other hand all verticals, upright and growing things such as rocks, trees, houses and people, are not shown from above at all but in approximately normal vision. A little of both ground plan and elevation is presented at the same time. In other words: we are seated in front of a deep stage on which the wings rise vertically above us whilst the stage floor, rising sharply as it recedes, permits a view from above.

The healthy Netherlandish sense of realism is less active in the whole than in the parts. In the details, such as the material texture of the rocks, a keen observation is at work, but the whole seems projected rather than perceived.

In more recent landscape painting it has become increasingly essential to be satisfied with such part of the landscape as happens to fall within a limited field of vision; in Patenier's day perspective dualism was a convention and a means of displaying nature with satisfactory clarity and in full detail.

Modern landscape painting is lyrical, Patenier's is epic. Love of nature had not yet crystallized out sufficiently clearly for everything, even the most secluded corners, to yield what modern sentimentality towards nature and art feels as 'atmosphere'. The lovers and buyers of Patenier's pictures were not satisfied with the effect as a whole, they wanted to read in the picture, they sought in it the leisure of a walk full of varied interest or a journey of discovery. If at every turn in the road they came upon adventure, discovered figures to interpret, relationships to trace, all the more satisfied did they feel.

Van Mander, in his life of Herri met de Bles, recounts already with a touch of irony how people would hunt for the owl in the painter's landscapes, how one would wager with another that he would not find it and how they idled away their time searching for the owl. 'Wondrously full of small details' is still praise from his lips.

What I have just indicated applies more to a fashion, a phase in

landscape painting, a tendency once predominant now odd, rather than
to an individual achievement. Patenier was certainly not the first to enter
this phase; he did not create a new category but he was its most distinguished representative who developed successfully and conspicuously,
as a specialist, what others had practised incidentally. In the victorious
progress of Netherlandish landscape painting no decisive step can be
associated with his name. He found no new relationships to nature. If he
was the first to regard himself as a professional landscape painter it was
because things had reached the point where such a profession became
possible. Jerome Bosch, who faced nature with greater subjectivity—and
not with the limitations of a specialist—fashioned his landscapes sketchily,
without emphasis, without display, but his point of view did not differ
from that of Patenier. He was a little older than Patenier and in the link,
if link there was, between the two masters he was certainly at the giving
end.

The features just emphasized cannot serve to define Patenier's *oeuvre*,
particularly since imitators exploited the successfully discovered formula.
His individual manner must be sought by less generalized, more detailed
observations.

184 The signed picture in Vienna, the *Baptism of Christ*, opens the way, but
it is in Madrid that Patenier's art is most effectively revealed in its full
scope, in four of his best pictures, including the two largest ones. To these
182 can be added a *St. Christopher* in the Escorial, but the unimportant though
185 genuinely signed pictures at Karlsruhe and Antwerp must serve as a
warning not to count too heavily on the Spanish experience.

Love of nature and self-abandon, and all the other virtues of our
landscape painters, did not suffice for Patenier, he required the wise
economy and measured skill of the architect. The imaginative power
that can set up a continent instinct with life is comparable to the creative
talent of an architect. Patenier divides to rule and does so systematically.
All the essential formations in his landscapes are presented parallel to
the picture plane, receding layer by layer into the depth, each rising a
little above the preceding one. They are so selected or rather so placed
as to present expressive profiles. The terrain is divided into strips that run
horizontally. It is not unusual for this system of parallel strips to be
continued in the clouds in the sky. Sharply rising rocks and tree trunks,
often with their roots in front, towering above the high-lying horizon,
intersecting all the ground lines at right angles, heighten the illusion of
space and help to divide the one scene into many scenes.

The general resources of perspective are used with assurance even though the construction is inconsistent in that, as I have explained, a single viewpoint from above is not adhered to. Recession is achieved by careful diminution with many gradations in the size of familar things such as houses, trees, and figures. An exaggerated and schematic use is made of aerial perspective in separating two grounds, the warm tones of the foreground, in which the heavy green of late summer predominates, and the cool blue transparent background. The pictures are often painted in two abruptly contrasting colours.

To our eyes Patenier's compositions show over-abundant signs of human activity. A system of straight lines, like the linear network of a map, is imposed on the picturesque freedom and fortuitousness of the landscape. The confusion and endlessness of nature is controlled by a fixed system which, however, never becomes unpleasantly rigid. A lively fantasy supplies manifold variety within the framework, and the details are so vivid that we gain confidence in the realism of the whole. We are captivated by the illusion that emanates from the individual parts and led to believe in the potential existence of the whole.

The *Rest on the Flight into Egypt* in the Prado is a mature masterpiece. 181 From the plants in the foreground, studied with loving insight and botanical accuracy, to the dusky masses of foliage in the middle ground, from the fancifully constructed Romanesque temple buildings to the blue distance, everything is scrupulously worked out, abundant and rich. The principal figure, the Madonna in a light cloak, firmly outlined but with a softly flowing line, seems a little out of keeping with the whole.

A powerful mood is emitted from this panel; though descriptive and didactic, it seems imbued with poetry. And we gain a similar impression from the *Temptation of St. Anthony* in the Prado and from the *St. Christopher* 180, 182 in the Escorial. But we are not entitled to regard the uniformly sonorous accord of the all-embracing chiaroscuro of the foliage and the luminous distance as the general characteristic of Patenier's art but must rather be content to discern his more intellectual virtues. Patenier differs from his imitators in the clarity of his compositions with their relatively strong contrasts of dark and light patches, in the pleasant objectivity and accuracy of the details. Thanks to his feeling for organic growth he himself never succumbed to the danger of light-hearted massing and overcrowding of detail, an inherent danger with this kind of landscape painting.

Steep, naked, sharp-edged, jagged rocks shooting up singly or in groups, and comfortably rounded, dense, dark masses of foliage are as it were the expressive features in the face of Patenier's landscape. His compositions can be classified according as to whether foliage or rocks predominate. In pictures of the Virgin the accent is on the tree, in representations of St. Jerome, and wherever the ascetic life of saints is portrayed, the expression is concentrated in the rocks. Patenier draws the grandeur of inhospitable mountain ranges into the devotional picture by exposing the contrast between the overwhelming power of the inanimate and the frailty of mankind. Man and the works of man seem lost. The buildings nestle in the crevices of the rocks and seek shelter there. Whereas in the *Baptism of Christ* in Vienna, the sudden alternations of water and rock produce an effect of vastness and desolation, all terrors of the mountains are piled on to the towering heights in the *St. Jerome* belonging to Mr. H. Oppenheimer, London,[1] which appears to be only the remaining half of a picture. The threatening mood is intensified by the heavy thunder clouds that cover one side of the sky and against which the jagged rocks stand off in bright relief.

Patenier's activity in Antwerp lasted barely ten years. According to the guild lists—in as far as they have been preserved and published—he had no pupils during this period. But even if not directly by teaching, he certainly influenced his contemporaries and compatriots in other ways. His modern style set a fashion which, in one way or another, was followed by almost everyone.

Seeing that Patenier, as van Mander relates and we observe, collaborated with other painters, his background landscape came to be considered as the background landscape *par excellence*. The model made the round of the workshops; imitation was made easy. If an artist of the standing of Quentin Massys collaborated with Patenier, then the lesser artists were certainly impelled to seek the aid of the landscape painter or to imitate what brought him so much success.

Quentin Massys is named as one of the guardians of Patenier's daughters, a proof of the friendship that must have existed between the two masters. In several of his landscapes Cornelis Massys, one of Quentin's sons, appears as a follower of Patenier. In a book on the Bruges Loan Exhibition of 1902 (Plate 67), I published the *St. Jerome* panel belonging to Mr. Brabandere, Thourout[2]; a similar picture, also signed, is in the Amalienstift, Dessau.[3] Cornelis was presumably still young when Patenier died. The picture at Thourout is dated 1547.

Patenier collaborated with the Master of the Female Half-Lengths.

187

*[1] Now in the National Gallery, London. According to Friedländer, *Die Altniederländische Malerei*, IX, 1931, p. 158, the picture is a replica of the left half of a painting in the Elberfeld Museum.

*[2] Now in the Royal Museum, Antwerp.

*[3] Later in the Dessau Museum.

Incidentally, in view of the difficulty that has arisen in locating this master, the fact provides a strong argument in favour of Antwerp. A picture of the *Virgin* in Copenhagen shows in the landscape the work of Patenier whilst the figures are by the anonymous master, an observation due to the keen eye of K. Madsen.

The case is not an isolated one. In the National Gallery, London, there is a *St. John on Patmos* in which I am also able to detect the hands of both masters. It seems to me that in the *Adoration of the Kings* by the Master of the Female Half-Lengths, in Munich,[1] the landscape was added by Patenier[2].    190

Patenier's relationship to Joos van Cleve is far more complicated. Van Mander's remark is a perpetual challenge to search for a picture showing the collaboration of the two painters. C. Justi has drawn attention to a *Madonna in a Landscape* in the Brussels gallery in which the figure is by   201 Joos (that is by the Master of the Death of the Virgin)—this is certain— and the landscape possibly by Patenier. It is at least in the 'manner of Patenier'. Moreover the clumsy conspicuousness of the luggage of the Holy Family is almost in the nature of a signature. Admittedly, the wicker basket is a well-known requisite of David's atelier, but in Patenier's workshop the luggage is supplemented by travel bags slung over Joseph's staff lying on the ground. So far so good and we might even be tempted to identify the Brussels picture with the one Van Mander saw. But an obstacle arises in the fact that elsewhere, too, in Joos's compositions the landscape is similarly conceived and has the same constituents. I cannot venture to establish the boundary line. Perhaps Patenier often collaborated with Joos, yet it seems more probable that Joos successfully appropriated the landscape painter's tricks.

If we are ever on the alert to find figures by other hands in Patenier's compositions we may eventually gain some idea of Patenier's own figure style from what remains. A dry, hesitant style leaning heavily on Quentin's art recurs and can be found nowhere outside Patenier's landscapes. To mention only the comparatively large and informative figures the ones in the Vienna *Baptism of Christ*, the Madonna in the excellent painting in Madrid, the *St. Christopher* in the Escorial and the unusual figures of saints that take up most of the picture plane in the altarpiece— destroyed by fire—of the von Kaufmann Collection in Berlin, these figures are not inconsistent with one another.

Patenier certainly needed help in his figure drawing. Just as he obtained

---

[1] Later transferred to the Germanisches Museum, Nürnberg, now in the Regensburg museum.

[2] Friedländer later reached the conclusion that in the paintings of the Master of the Female Half-Lengths the landscapes were mostly his own work, done in imitation of Patenier's style (see Friedländer, *Die Altniederländische Malerei*, IX, 1931, p. 121, and XII, 1935, p. 27).

a study sheet with St. Christopher designs from Albrecht Dürer he may also have borrowed from Quentin Massys and other artists.

In his relatively archaic manner, which seems poised mid-way between Bosch and Massys, Patenier develops the figures relief-like in layers running parallel to the picture plane and likes to form the contours with long unbroken lines of little amplitude and sometimes haltingly; he arranges the drapery with understanding and taste, and in general is content to get round difficulties. The expression is always concentrated in the landscape, on which the master obviously dwells with greater pleasure and more freedom.

Patenier's stimulating influence made itself felt in the circle of Bruges artists. Far-reaching conclusions have been drawn from the fact that in 1515, in the same year as Patenier, a Gerard of Bruges—none other, as we believe, than Gerard David—became master at Antwerp. But far clearer than the landscape painter's link with David is his relationship 191–192 with the painter whom we call Adriaen Ysenbrandt. At least one joint work by Ysenbrandt and Patenier survives in a *Flight into Egypt* belonging to Mr. A. Thiem in San Remo.[1]

The following dates are of importance: even before 1500 David's landscape style was essentially established and thereafter evolved organically; Ysenbrandt became master at Bruges in 1510, Patenier went to Antwerp in 1515. I am inclined to view the situation as follows (always provided that the so-called 'Waagen Mostaert' is really identical with Ysenbrandt): prior to 1515 Patenier had spent a shorter or longer period at Bruges; in his relationship with the rather older Gerard David he was the one to be influenced, but Ysenbrandt, completely dominated though he was by David, sought now and again to profit from Patenier's art.

The moment we take Gerard David and Jerome Bosch into consideration Patenier's achievement appears limited. We cannot credit the first landscape painter with a single new discovery but we can discern in him a prophetic intuition of the value of this new field of art, which he cultivated with such devotion. Not only did Patenier make landscape predominant, he made it resound and—within the limits of descriptive landscape—imbued it with idyllic sentiment and pathos that touches our emotions.

*[1] Later in the Robert T. Francis Collection, New York.—In Friedländer's later view the landscape is only 'in the manner of Patenier', see *Die Altniederländische Malerei*, XI, 1933, p. 132.

# JOOS VAN CLEVE

THERE are sound arguments to support the hypothesis that the Master of the Death of the Virgin is identical with Joos van Cleve. The personality was constructed entirely from stylistic criticism and has taken full shape. But from the name alone we can establish a few dates and with them the framework for a biography. Joos became master at Antwerp in 1511 and seems to have lived there until his death in 1540. Entries in the Antwerp lists for 1511, 1516, 1519, 1523, 1525, 1535, 1536 confirm his presence there; the long gap between 1525 and 1535 is striking, and the possibility that he was absent from Antwerp for a considerable time must be borne in mind.[1] C. Justi, in his clear-sighted and comprehensive way, studied the arguments in favour of the identification, first put forward by Firmenich-Richartz, but he did not reach a satisfactory conclusion.[2]

The arms of the dukes of Cleve which appear on a dog collar in the altarpiece of the *Adoration of the Kings* in the Naples museum provide us with an important piece of evidence. Whether Joos was born at Cleves or belonged to a family that had been settled for generations in Antwerp is immaterial, and in any case the arms could indicate his origin or his name, always provided that it is not an allusion to the donor of the altarpiece, a possibility that Justi did not overlook.

Quite recently an exact and careful replica of the triptych has come to light in the Emden Collection (sale in Berlin, later the property of Mr. van Gelder, Uccle near Brussels[3]). And here the coat of arms on the dog 196 collar has been duly copied. As it is improbable that both versions were done for the same patron we can with increased confidence link the coat of arms with the artist or the workshop. Moreover there is a second escutcheon in the Naples picture, a cross on light ground the lower part of which seems to terminate in an anchor.

Guicciardini relates that Joos van Cleve was such an excellent portraitist that he was called to Paris by the French king François I to paint portraits. His actual words are: *Gios di Cleves cittadino d'Anversa rarissimo*

---

*[1] The gap has been slightly narrowed down by the discovery that in 1528 Joos bought a house in Antwerp (cf. Friedländer, *Die Altniederländische Malerei*, IX, 1931, p. 23).

[2] In *Jahrbuch der preussichen Kunstsammlungen*, XVI, pp. 13 ff.

*[3] Now in the Institute of Arts, Detroit.

*nel colorire, & tanto eccelente nel ritrarre dal naturale, che havendo il Re Francesco primo mandati qua huomini a posta, per condurre alla Corte qualche maestro egregio, costui fu l'eletto, & condotto in Francia ritrasse il Re, & la Regina, & altri Principi con somma laude & premi grandissimi.* It has been suggested that the Antwerp historian committed the error of confusing Joos van Cleve with Jean Clouet; there has also been much speculation as to whether the entry did not refer to the younger Joos van Cleve (who has recently been almost obliterated by the art critics)[1]. But in my opinion portraits of the French king and of his wife exist which clearly reveal the style of the Master of the Death of the Virgin and this seems to me to confirm the statement of Guicciardini and to provide the best argument in favour of the identification.

There are a great many portraits of François I, most of which in contour and technique show the uninspired slickness and convention of the Clouet workshop. Several of the king's portraits, however, are conspicuous for greater breadth and more lively gestures and are based on the conception of a master with a different outlook. Here, as always when we are dealing with portraits of royalty, replicas, copies, variations exist, and as we are seaching for the author of the original model, the one painted from life, we must pay more attention to the composition than to the execution.

At Hampton Court there is a portrait of the king, of indifferent quality (with the old number 330), that is attributed to Joos van Cleve in the inventories. The same type recurs in a version—without hands formerly in the Doetsch Collection (Sale, London 1895, No. 184)—and in one of considerably superior workmanship in the Johnson Collection, Philadelphia. In the American picture the head, the hat, the left hand are similar to the Hampton Court version but the right hand is in a different position and the costume shows variations, in Philadelphia a carefully reproduced state robe of individual character. The portrait in the Johnson Collection could be an original by the Master of the Death of the Virgin; to prove our point it would be sufficient to establish that it goes back to an original by this artist.[2]

A series of portraits of Eleanor, wife of the French king, survive, all suggesting one prototype. Again we can distinguish between various versions which show deviations in the costume and in the hands. A good example, at one time in the Minutoli Collection, was acquired for the

---

[1] The so-called Joos van Cleve the Younger has been convincingly identified with Cornelis van Cleve ("Sotte Clef") by L. Burchard (in *Mélanges Hulin de Loo*, 1931, pp. 53 ff.). See also Friedländer, *Die Altniederländische Malerei*, IX, 1931, p. 21, and XIV, 1937, pp. 115 ff., and again in *Oud-Holland*, XL, 1943, pp. 7 f.

[2] In *Die Altniederländische Malerei*, IX, 1931, pp. 50 and 139, the Johnson version is accepted by Friedländer as an original work of Joos van Cleve.

VII · Lucas van Leyden · *The Adoration of the Kings* · Chicago, Art Institute

Kunsthistorisches Museum, Vienna. I do not doubt that this painting, 195
formerly erroneously ascribed to Jan Gossaert, if not an original by the
Master of the Death of the Virgin at least vouches for a lost original by
his hand.[1]

Incidentally the master seems to have specialized in royal portraits.
From his workshop came portraits of Emperor Maximilian (one bearing
the early date 1510) and also of Henry VIII (Hampton Court No. 563, 194
that must be dated about 1536, in old inventories under 'Jennet or Sotto
Cleve').

We are able to trace the master's work back a little further than 1511,
the date when he became free master at Antwerp. In addition to the
Emperor's portrait of 1510 (Musée Jacquemart-André, Paris), there are
two modest wings, *Adam and Eve*, dated 1507, in the Louvre—not in
perfect condition. I am inclined to accept these works as by our master
though they also recall Jan Joest of Haarlem, who worked at Kalkar
between 1504 and 1508. From this we could draw far-reaching conclusions. We might assume that Joos van Cleve, before he went to Antwerp,
worked at Kalkar, perhaps in collaboration with the Haarlem master.
The fact that Barthel Bruyn, who was born in 1493, to judge from the
style of his early works, was a third member of the group lends itself to
further speculations. Joos van Cleve was presumably a little older than
Bruyn and younger than Jan Joest. It is almost certain that Bruyn was a
pupil of Jan Joest (presumably not at Kalkar but in Haarlem).

In 1515, the very year in which Barthel Bruyn, whose art was entirely
dependent on Jan Joest, began to work at Cologne, the brothers Hackenay
commisioned the two altarpieces with the *Death of the Virgin* from Joos
van Cleve. The smaller triptych in the Wallraf-Richartz Museum, 197–198
Cologne, is dated 1515, the larger one (Munich Pinakothek), must have
been done immediately after, seeing that the donor portraits are unchanged
(Nicasius Hackenay died as early as 1518).

A *Virgin and Child with St. Bernard*, bequeathed to the Louvre some
years ago, of good quality though it has attracted little attention, seems
considerably more archaic than the *Death of the Virgin* in Cologne. The
*Descent from the Cross* in the Dresden gallery, in part dependent on the
Master of Flémalle, is even more hesitant, almost the work of a beginner,
though, admittedly, it is not so evidently a work by Joos.

Among his earliest portraits is the one of a *Young Woman* in the Musée
Mayer van Bergh, Antwerp.

*[1] According to Friedländer (*Die Altniederländische Malerei*, IX, 1931, pp. 27 and 143) the Vienna
version is an exact replica by the master, equal in quality to the original, which is at Hampton
Court.

The *Death of the Virgin* provides the best starting-point for the period around 1515. The smaller *Adoration of the Kings* at Dresden may have been done a little earlier.

193    The *Portrait of a Woman* in Florence is dated 1520. Many other works can be fitted in here. The altarpiece with the *Lamentation over Christ* in the Staedel Institute, Frankfurt, dates from 1524. The traditional date is reliable. Not much later, in my opinion, is the large *Adoration of the Kings* at Dresden whilst the altarpiece, formerly at Genoa now in the Louvre,

202    with the *Lamentation over Christ* and, on the predella, the *Last Supper*, inspired by Leonardo, may date from about 1530. The self-portraits that have been detected in the two *Adorations* in Dresden and in the Louvre altarpiece assist us to fix these dates. A stay at Genoa, where at one time at least three altarpieces by the master stood—the *Crucifixion* in the Thiem Collection,[1] the *Adoration of the Kings* in S. Donato and the altarpiece now in the Louvre—is very probable.

Joos van Cleve remained quietly aloof from experimental or pioneer work. He practised his art efficiently and successfully with a workshop that tended to turn out rather factory-like products, and his relationship with his contemporaries was pleasantly harmonious. As he was directly or indirectly influenced by Leonardo he presumably considered himself progressive but his modernism is superficial. He did not lag behind and modified his mode of expression but the change does not touch the core of his art. Beginning and end lie close together, at least for a painter of this period.

160–163    Bernaert van Orley, perhaps less talented but more assiduous and restless, did not pause for long where Joos was content to linger. Successful not only in Antwerp but also at Cologne, Genoa, Paris, Joos saw no reason to make decisive changes. His attractive manner, never prickly, with few contrasts, and a readily accessible gay prettiness gave him easy success. His rosy creatures feel equally at home in bright interiors or park-like landscapes. As opposed to the proud aloofness which Quentin Massys, whose gold he often changes into baser coin, infuses into his holy persons, Joos makes his creatures sociable and companionable.

His adroit adoption and assimilation of the motifs of others is not perhaps the best testimony for deep-seated originality. The following survey may prove instructive:

After Jan van Eyck (*Madonna* in Frankfurt): Collection of Mr.
204    Spiridon, Paris.[2]

*[1] Now in the Metropolitan Museum of Art, New York.
*[2] Now in the Metropolitan Museum of Art, New York.

After Rogier van der Weyden (*Descent from the Cross*, Escorial): with landscape added, Johnson Collection, Philadelphia.

After the Master of Flémalle (*Descent from the Cross*, cf. the copy in Liverpool): the Dresden *Descent from the Cross*.

After Gerard David (*Madonna in Half-Length*): American art market.[1]

After Quentin Massys (*Salvator Mundi*): Louvre and elsewhere.

After the Master of the Morrison Triptych (an Angel in the Morrison triptych): In the *Madonna* at Ince Hall near Liverpool.[2]

200

After Albrecht Dürer (*St. Jerome*): Endless replicas showing more or less clearly the style of Joos.

After Leonardo (the group of embracing children, Christ and St. John): several replicas.

After Leonardo (*Madonna with the Cherries*): Several replicas, a good one at Schloss Meiningen.

Presumably there was a direct contact with the art of Leonardo, particularly if Joos really worked for a time in Paris. Leonardo, it is true, died in 1519 and we have good grounds for believing that the Antwerp master was not called to Paris until later but there was certainly still much talk at the French court about the Italian genius and there would be many of his works to show. There, too, was Andrea Solario, a Milanese artist of lesser stature, who comes astonishingly close to the Master of the Death of the Virgin.

In spite of his readiness to borrow motifs, the master's inventive powers were not indolent. His imagination, though not creative, was lively enough to push bodies adroitly around. A nimble mind was needed to create successfully from the same types and in the same spirit two compositions as widely divergent as the representations of the *Death of the Virgin* in Cologne and Munich. The slim figures are inordinately active. 197–198 Their flurry and commotion impairs the dignity of the scene. The excessive reduction of scale in the figures in the background makes the space appear wide and not clearly defined. A more profound effect is not achieved, particularly as the coldly gleaming, rather sugary colouring interspersed with strong red, so characteristic for the artist, seems unsuitable for the subject.

If anywhere, Joos is independent when depicting the mother joys of the Virgin Mary. Joseph shares her happiness like a benevolent grandpapa. The attractive *Madonnas* and *Holy Families* were a success. There are a

[1] Now in the Metropolitan Museum of Art, New York.
[2] Now at Lulworth Castle, Dorset.

large number of replicas, imitations and copies. The boldest conception
203 can be seen in the version in the Fitzwilliam Museum, Cambridge. The
Virgin smiles as she looks down on the Child asleep at her breast. This
sensuous, blissful smile does not come from Heaven and conceals no
secret; on the contrary, it is sure of general approval and of making an
immediate appeal. Where he is idyllic and sentimental, of gay, festive
mood the master readily attains an easy goal but the tearful Passion
scenes appear languid.

In the portraits, especially the early ones, the face is conspicuous as a
bright blob, with the hair, the hat and the clothing forming a dark frame.
The wide-open eyes look out piercingly dark from the bright disk, which
as a whole has little solidity. In later portraits the head is more powerfully
modelled. The schematic drawing of the profile line in three-quarter
view is interesting. The critical point is near the eye where the part
between eyelid and brows seems pushed out so that the line of the cheek
is interrupted and does not merge directly into the line of the forehead.
The upper eyelid runs approximately parallel with the lower one so that
where it terminates in the nose it has to be brought down steeply to the
strongly emphasized lachrymal gland. The later portraits are larger in
size than the earlier ones, they show fat, boneless, almost swollen forms
and dull expressions.

# JAN PROVOST

ACCORDING to documents brought to light by James Weale, Jan
Provost came from Mons, a town in the Southern Netherlands
lying close to the present French frontier, not far from Valenciennes and Maubeuge. It would seem, so Hulin hints, that Weale found a
trace of the master at Valenciennes.[1] But confirmation for this is still
outstanding. Provost, who appears to have been born in 1462, and is thus
not younger than Quentin Massys, attempted to gain a footing in Antwerp
two years later than Quentin Massys, namely in 1493, in which year he
is entered as master in the guild lists of the town ('Jan Provoost'). But in
1494 he became master at Bruges, where he remained until his death in
1529. It is certainly not his origin and schooling that justify us in
reckoning him to the Bruges masters but rather his long and successful
activity in the Flemish city.

When Provost settled at Bruges, Memlinc was the representative of the
recognized school but for the younger generation, and certainly for the
painters who had come via Antwerp, a representative of an out-moded
and old-fashioned style. Gerard David belonged to the same generation
as Provost. The newcomer had to establish himself successfully alongside
David, whose art seemed relatively archaic and bound by ecclesiastic
convention.

With Provost a worldly, turbulent spirit penetrates from the South to
the musty cloistral calm of Bruges. Antwerp was the centre to which the
younger talents flocked from every part of the Netherlands where, less
oppressed by tradition than at Bruges, they could exchange ideas freely
and promote rapid innovations. Provost seems to have kept up his relations with Antwerp. At least when Dürer was there in 1520 Provost was
there too, made contact with the Nuremberg artist and accompanied him
to Bruges on April 6th, 1521.

By a fortunate chance the *Last Judgement* painted by Provost in 1525, **207**
for the Bruges Town Hall, has escaped destruction.[2] This panel was the

*[1] At Valenciennes before 1491, Provost married the widow of Simon Marmion, Jeanne de
Quaronbe. He is said to have become a burgess of Valenciennes in 1498. See Friedländer, *Die
Altniederländische Malerei*, IX, 1931, p. 74.

*[2] Parts of the picture, showing clerics in hell, were repainted by P. Pourbus in 1549/50. These
repaintings were removed in 1956.

starting-point for research on Provost. It enabled us to detect the hand of the master in several other panels. Although Provost did not put his signature to any work, stylistic criticism has been able to resurrect his personality successfully. The picture that gave us the first idea of the artist's style was done during his last years and what could be added as the first fruits of stylistic criticism belongs to the same, that is the last, phase of his development. Our immediate task, therefore, seeing that the long interval between 1493 and 1525 remains empty, is to search for works belonging to earlier periods.

206    Hulin and I began by recognizing the *Madonna with the Angels, Prophets and Sibyls* in St. Petersburg as a second work by Provost. The panel, more than 6 ft. in height, came from the collection of King William of Holland and was sold in 1850 as a Quentin Massys for 2000 fl. It was transferred from wood to canvas, in the process of which it lost some of its freshness and luminosity. Hulin connects it with a document of 1524 which contains a reference to an altar panel painted by Provost for S. Donatian, Bruges (for an altar dedicated to the prophet Daniel).

In conjunction with the *Last Judgement* at Bruges, the painting in St. Petersburg is most informative. The evidence from the two works is complementary and agrees. The compositions are pleasant, far removed from the solemn monumentality of David, are gay and festive and light in colour. The rather monotonous ideal types are fashioned with an eye for sensuous qualities. The women, including the sibyls, are youthful with well-rounded forms, large mouths with faintly smiling lips, the prophets are strikingly youthful with long beards that often seem stuck on. The general effect is agreeable and lively in form but shallow and empty in spirit. In addition to the authenticated *Last Judgement* we have no less than three other versions of the same subject by the master.

1. Weber Collection, Hamburg, now Kunsthalle, Hamburg.
2. Nieuwenhuys Sale, Brussels 1883, No. 1 (Aeken)—23 × 24¼ in., now in the Institute of Arts, Detroit, U.S.A.
3. Vicomte de Ruffo Collection, Brussels. Exhibited Bruges, 1902, No. 169.

It was the task of painting the *Last Judgement* in particular that was entrusted to our master because of all the Bruges painters of his generation it was he who had imagination and, comparatively speaking, showed the greatest boldness in his treatment of the nude. Whilst the pictures in Hamburg and Detroit appear to be roughly contemporary versions, with only slight deviations from the 1525 picture, the replica in the Vicomte de Ruffo Collection is more archaic in structure, less personal in the types, dry, stiff and (if the attribution is correct) must be regarded as considerably earlier than Provost's *Last Judgement* of 1525.

To proceed direct to the de Ruffo panel is difficult and hardly permissible without intermediary stages. However little developed Provost's formal language appears to be in the hands and the female types of the de Ruffo panel and however far removed the disposition with the limited number of persons and the isolation of the figures seems from the closely intertwined groups in the other *Judgement* panels, the heads of the men with their black eyebrows and thick lips and the movements of the nude figures appear to some extent characteristic for Provost.

There is, however, another way which leads us to the earlier phases of the known Provost style. A *Lamentation over Christ* sold with the estate of G. Ferroni (March 1909, 'Memlinc') is certainly a work by our master. The picture is now in the von Back Collection in Szegedin.[1] Here in particular Mary Magdalen kneeling on the left is characteristic enough in type. To this archaic work various Passion panels can be linked one by one, becoming increasingly remote from the accustomed Provost style.

1. Sale Schevitch (Paris 1906, *Pietà* with St. Mary Magdalen and St. John).[2]
2. Madrid, Photo Laurent No. 2630, *Pietà*, similar in composition to the foregoing.
3. Paris, Kleinberger, *Pietà* with full-length figures.[3]
4. Madrid, private Collection, *Adoration of Kings*.

I think that with this group I have established something of Provost's early style (1490–1500). The expression of grief is strong but monotonous. The mouth is wide and straight. The eyes are deep-set, narrow and dark. The grouping is archaic with a relatively advanced treatment of the nude that heralds the softness and mellowness of the later style.

In his compositions Provost is more enterprising than reflective. Lavish groupings result in over-crowding, an unclear spatial effect, the jarring proximity of large and small figures and an uncertainty in the proportions —with stumpy figures next to inordinately long ones. In two altar wings that form a pair— *St. Catherine Disputing* (Rotterdam) and the *Martyrdom* of that saint in the Antwerp museum—from the artist's late and best-known period, the inadequacies have been frankly used to give a naive

---

*[1] Later (between 1930 and 1946) on the London art market.
*[2] The painting turned up again at a sale at Charpentier's, Paris, 1 June 1949 (lot 56).
*[3] Now in the Boveri Collection, Zurich.

205 and boldly grotesque effect, whereas simple tasks such as the Madonnas
at Cremona and Piacenza are boldly conceived and the soft prettiness of
the female heads does not fail to appeal.

I should like to add here a few small observations on superficial things
because, though they may not help us to make an attribution, they can
at least help to check attributions. Provost loved landscapes planned like
gardens (flower-pots, espaliers, flower beds); he avoided distant views
and wide vistas. He frequently gave the Virgin a ring on her finger, a
motif that, as far as I know, was not used by any other Netherlandish
artist of the period.

Attention should be paid to the shape of the hand, which, at any rate
in the late period, is a sure criterion for the artist. The fingers are long with
flexible joints, angular rather than arched, with the finger joints inclined
at an angle. On the inside of the hand the fingers are sharply divided
from the palm by a continuous straight line. Evidently the master prided
himself on an elegant, well-articulated hand.

The full mouth with slightly protruding lower lip and deep-set eyes
are the most reliable characteristics for Provost's fairly constant female
types.

Provost's personality, more imaginative than vigorous, is not easy to
grasp because in his anxiety to please he does not remain untouched by
the changing fashions that appear in Antwerp. He is stimulated in
particular by Quentin Massys, whose melodious drapery flow he strives
to imitate. In talent and taste he is at least the equal of Joos van Cleve
but he did not exploit his ability as efficiently as the Antwerp artist.

# JAN GOSSAERT

THE masters who represent the sixteenth century for us differ considerably amongst themselves. A common background is now of less consequence than before. Each one, at least of the more talented artists, thrusts forward on his own initiative. More through the ability to combine and blend than as a result of creative power works are produced simultaneously on Netherlandish soil that have but little in common.

In the general atmosphere of unrest and discontent several assiduous painters are driven from one direction to another by changing fashions. The entity of personality is submerged in the profusion of new ideals and models that pour in from all sides. In the case of Orley, the art critic, assisted by only a small number of works authenticated by inscriptions, finds it difficult to get his bearings, in the case of Lucas van Leyden he has to make continual changes in rapid succession. To follow Jan Gossaert on his way is comparatively easy.

A substantial number of signed panels by his hand, some of them also dated, are easily accessible in the great galleries of London, Paris, Berlin, Munich and Vienna. Furthermore his language is loud, decided and, at bottom, unchanging, not easy to mistake. We are assisted by the fact that Gossaert never allowed his pupils to collaborate in his own work and that everything he produced, as a result of his ambition, his assiduity and his outstanding skill, possesses a quality that is hard to imitate.

What we know of Gossaert's life flows from van Mander's pen but it has unfortunately not been possible to add much to this information from other sources.

Gossaert came from Maubeuge in the Hainaut, now part of France. Hence his name Mabuse and the form of name he favoured for his signature at a later period: 'Joannes Malbodius'. The date of his birth is not known, he was probably born between 1470 and 1480 and was thus a contemporary of Dürer, a little younger than Quentin Massys, a little older than Lucas van Leyden.

An important clue has been found in the lists of the Antwerp St. Luke's Guild, in which for the year 1503 'Jennyn van Hennegouwe' is entered as master. It has been rightly assumed that this refers to Jan Gossaert, particularly as he wrote his name at least on two occasions in a similar way (JENNINE and GENNIN). Mr. J. Masson of Amiens owns a circular drawing[1] with the *Beheading of John the Baptist*, bearing the genuine inscription: GENNIN.GOSSART.DE.M. The name in a similar form is also found on a panel with the *Adoration of the Kings* acquired by the National Gallery, London, from the Carlisle Collection.

223

The next date is 1508. In that year Gossaert accompanied his patron Philip of Burgundy to Rome. Philip went as ambassador to Italy. A stay in the South in the service of a prince with wide humanistic interests offered opportunities for the artist similar to those that were later offered to the artist Jan van Scorel of Utrecht. Antiquity was the ideal, sculpture and the nude figure the centre of interest. And an echo of it resounds throughout his entire artistic production. If his conception seems sculptural, this preference, if not produced, must at any rate have been strengthened by the Roman impressions. His biographer van Nimwegen says of Philip: *nihil magis eum Romae dilectabat, quam sacra illa vetustatis monumenta, quae per celeberrimum pictorem Joannem Gossardum Malbodium depingenda sibi curavit.*

I believe I am able to point out a drawing done by Gossaert in Rome in 1508 after an antique statue that was famous at the time, namely a carefully finished pen drawing in the Venice Academy (Scuola Tedesca, Photo Anderson) of the *Resting Apollo*, the so-called *Hermaphrodite*, which at the beginning of the sixteenth century was in the courtyard of the Casa Sassi. The statue, drawn also by Heemskerck, is now at Naples.[2]

210

In 1509 Gossaert returned from Italy but instead of settling again at Antwerp followed royal patrons all over the place. According to the Antwerp guild lists he registered pupils in 1505 and 1507. His name does not occur there again after 1507. Decisive for his manner was the patronage of highly placed personalities, legitimate or semi-legitimate scions of the Habsburg-Burgundian house. The 'exquisite' and virtuoso qualities of his paintings are explained by the fact that the rich patrons rewarded exceptional achievements. Like Jan van Eyck, Gossaert worked mainly in the services of princes, went everywhere and was equally little tied to the guild of any particular town. Unless van Mander was misinformed as to his character, Gossaert appears to have been arrogant and somewhat dissolute.

*[1] Now in the Ecole des Beaux-Arts, Paris.
*[2] Three more drawings done by Gossaert after Roman monuments are now known: The 'Spinario (Print Room of the University, Leyden), the Colosseum (Print Room, Berlin-Dahlem), and the Hercules, after the statue from the Forum Boarium, now in the Palazzo dei Conservatori, Rome (Lord Wharton, London).

Gossaert's main patron apart from Philip of Burgundy was the latter's son Adolph of Burgundy, whose residence was at Middelburg in Zeeland and who retained the painter there at least for a time. Further Jan Carondelet, whose portrait he seems to have painted three times, King 219 Christian II of Denmark, who had married a sister of the emperor Charles V, finally the regent Margaret. Presumably, apart from Antwerp the most important centres of his activity were: Bruges, because it was almost certainly Carondelet's headquarters, Brussels and Malines, because of the Habsburg court, Utrecht, because Philip of Burgundy settled there, and without doubt Middelburg, because it was Adolph's residence. Gossaert's chief work, most emphatically admired by van Mander, was at Middelburg: a very large *Descent from the Cross* (unfortunately destroyed), commissioned by Maximilian of Burgundy. In 1520 Dürer saw this work and gave his opinion of it as follows: *nit so gut im Hauptstreichen als im Gemäl*, by which he probably meant that it was not so good in the invention as in the execution. The painter seems to have died at Middelburg in 1533 or 1534.[1]

The earliest accredited and dated work by Gossaert is unfortunately relatively late, namely 1516. It is the panel in the Berlin gallery with the life-size nude figures of *Neptune and Amphitrite*, fully signed, painted for 213 Philip of Burgundy and bearing this patron's name and device. Strangely enough Gossaert borrowed the composition from Dürer's famous engraving of *Adam and Eve*.

By 1516 the master was in full possession of his mature style. This dated panel gives us just as little information about his beginnings and the origins of his art as do the works dated 1517, the diptych with the portrait of Carondelet in the Louvre and the *Hercules* panel in the Cook 219–220 Collection, Richmond.[2] The only other dated works we have are an engraving of 1522, the Hercules panel of 1523 (preserved only in a copy, on the Vienna art market) and works dated 1526 and 1527; nothing more after 1527. Stylistic criticism must come to our aid and can do so the more easily because several indubitable works by the master, though not inscribed with dates, were, to judge by their style, obviously done before 1516. Fortunately at least one of these works is signed, and owing to its outstanding importance and the eloquence of its language seems ideal as a point of departure. A few years ago this work was acquired by

---

*[1] 1532 is now established as the year of Gossaert's death by a document published by J. M. March (in *Boletin de la Sociedad Española de Excursiones*, LIII, 1949, p. 221). For details see also J. K. Steppe, in exhibition catalogue *Jan Gossaert, genoemd Mabuse*, Rotterdam and Bruges, 1965, pp. 33–8.
*[2] Now in the Barber Institute, Birmingham.

223    the National Gallery, London, from Lord Carlisle and has since been easily accessible.    Formerly, when it was at Castle Howard and at Naworth Castle, few art critics had been familiar with the stupendous achievement of this *Adoration of the Kings*. With a concealed but indisputable signature "IENNI. GOSSART. OG MABVS—" and in another place: "IENNIN GOS —" removing all doubt as to the authorship, the picture reveals its cold-hearted creator in quite a different relationship to tradition than van Mander's account would have led us to expect.[1]

Guicciardini and Vasari write: "Gossaert was the first (Vasari: *quasi il primo*) to bring the true method of representing nude figures and mythologies from Italy to the Netherlands." Van Mander read the eulogy and gladly used it in his vita of the master. Since then opinion everywhere has been guided accordingly, so that, depending on the writer's point of view, Gossaert is represented either as a great innovator or as the first mannerist and corrupter of art. Gossaert's relationship to Italian art is in so far rightly expressed in Vasari's sentence as Gossaert himself would have certainly recognized it as a just acknowledgement of his own intentions. Since we are not concerned with ambitions but with results, the accustomed ideas must be modified and altered. On two occasions we note that Gossaert, when he had to do nude figures, followed Dürer, once in the *Neptune* panel of 1516 and again in a wing of the triptych at Palermo. These observations are in contradiction to Vasari's phrase. Gossaert was not equal to the part allotted to him though it was certainly a role he would have liked to play. Without ability to compose freely he could not get very far with the 'true method'. He certainly found opportunity to appropriate Italian motifs. On occasion he would adorn the façade with foreign decorative elements but the foundation was too narrow to support the magnificent structure of a Netherlandish Renaissance. At bottom the master had assimilated nothing of Italian art beyond a preference for plastic form and a craving for nude bodies in violent movement. The moment it came to the crystallizing out of his forms he was dependent on the model, on ungainly reality.

223    In the Carlisle panel, in which the master strained his resources to the limit, he does not seem to have gone against tradition but he certainly did his utmost to surpass all previous achievements. From a superficial and uncritical examination it might appear that this ambitious goal had been attained. In the solidity of the painting, in the conscientiousness of the execution, in the characterization of the materials and in the rendering

---

[1] Cf. Friedländer, *Jan Gossaert (Mabuse)*: *The Adoration of the Kings in the National Gallery*. (The Gallery Books, No. 19). London 1948.

of all still-life-like details Gossaert's work, it is true, is not inferior to anything in the fifteenth century, but it is not imbued with life, lacks the joyous abandon, the eager participation in the action without which, at bottom, no work can rise above the level of a virtuosity of craftsmanship. The *Adoration of the Kings* is shown as a court ceremony. There is a complete lack of dramatic movement, and relationships between the individual, stiffly parading figures are scarcely established. Gossaert's talent lacks dynamism. Self-conscious in expression, he is timid in composition, with only few ideas, and as a draughtsman he is sure of himself only when a life-model is continuously available, otherwise, particularly in fore-shortening, at any rate in his early period, he is unreliable. The fact that the two dogs in the foreground that seem so completely realistic are borrowed, and most adroitly borrowed, from engravings by Dürer and Schongauer is symptomatic and instructive.

The *Adoration of the Kings* probably dates from about 1506.[1] The master, who was so firmly linked to the Netherlandish tradition, later made a great show of his thirst for modernity. He was revolutionary in will rather than in talent. Right to the end his painting remained solid and firm. The enamel-like purity of the material, the light fluency of the brushwork, adhered to even when conflicting with the strenuously sought monumentality of the drawing, remained intact and that at a time when technique was disrupted on all sides. Of his predecessors Gossaert certainly admired van Eyck, and the study of Eyckian works had assuredly formed part of his training. He took the three principal figures God the Father, the Virgin and St. John, from the Ghent altarpiece and varied them skilfully. His adaptation, in half-lengths, is in the Prado; it is unsigned. The convincing attribution was made by Scheibler. A comparison with the original reveals the mannered undulations of Gossaert's formal style. Nevertheless it remains a masterpiece of archaizing composition. Gossaert has added an angel of his own invention but the difference in style is in no way obtrusive. The picture in Madrid is by no means a particularly early work. The Gothic elements in the ornamental frame, a goldsmith Gothic run wild, must not be put forward as a decisive argument that Gossaert painted the panel before his journey to Italy. It is true that after that journey he generally used Renaissance elements. But since his interest in architecture and ornament was determined not by feeling or inclination or taste but by calculating knowledge, he was able to use one or other form according to the inclination of the moment. On the whole he follows naturally the

*[1]For the date see p. 102, note 1

contemporary taste that proceeds from a rich painterly Gothic to a bare
Renaissance style.

The *Malvagna* triptych in the museum at Palermo is of earlier date
222 than the picture in the Prado and approximately contemporary with the
*Adoration of the Kings* in the National Gallery. More modest in size than
the Carlisle panel, it is pitched in a lower key and the masterly execution
has produced a jewel of scintillating, sparkling brilliance. In the type of
Madonna and in the rolling undulating play of the drapery, in the
metallic-like fineness and precision of the Gothic ornament the personal
style of the artist is revealed at a height that no imitator could hope to
attain. But once again we catch the master borrowing. The group of
Adam and Eve on the (left) wing is taken from Dürer's woodcut (from the
*Little Passion*).[1] Around 1520 the triptych was copied more than once in
the Netherlands. At that time it was presumably at Bruges. The painter
known as Adriaen Ysenbrandt, a Bruges painter, used it at least three
times (the central panel, translated into the rather languid manner of
this David imitator, formerly Frau von Kaufmann Collection, Berlin,[2]
and Baron de Rothschild Collection, Paris, the wing with Adam and
Eve formerly Emden Collection, Hamburg[3]). Gossaert's triptych is said
to have been at Messina about 1600. It so happens that Jan Carondelet,
one of Gossaert's famous patrons, who was Chancellor of Flanders and
certainly lived for a time at Bruges, was also Bishop of Palermo. It is
therefore very tempting to assume that he owned the work at Bruges and
later donated it to Sicily.

The *Agony in the Garden* in the Kaiser Friedrich Museum, Berlin, with
224 the consistent treatment of the moonlight (the motif stimulated the artist
to a veritable *tour de force*) and the curiously unsuccessful heads, is one
of his earlier works. Whereas in those tasks that called for free compositional powers and the invention of figure types Gossaert failed to make
the grade, from his youth on he was a striking portraitist and excelled in
expressing imperious manhood, which was always greatly appreciated
by his contemporaries. In the Carlisle panel the portrait or portrait-like
heads are the best part and provide a good starting point for tracing other
contemporary, i.e. early, single portraits. I regard, with varying degrees
of certainty, a few male portraits from the period around 1510 as works
by Gossaert. These include the clear-cut *Head of a Young Man* in the Cook

*[1] This fact led Friedländer (in *Die Altniederländische Malerei*, VIII, pp. 17 ff.) to date the
Malvagna triptych and the National Gallery *Adoration c.* 1512, as Dürer's *Passion* bears the dates
1509–1511.
*[2] Now in the von Pannwitz Collection.
*[3] Sold with the E. Weinberger collection, Vienna, 22 October 1929.

Collection, Richmond[1] (with the painted stone frame that the master 216
favoured so greatly), the stern, tense *Head of an Old Man* in Baron von
Liphart's Collection at Ratshof[2] and a *Portrait of a Man* in the Copenhagen
gallery.

The *St. Luke painting the Virgin*, originally at Malines, now in the Prague
gallery, occupies an intermediary position. It probably dates from about 214
1515. Fortunately it is signed. Otherwise the question of its authorship
would be difficult, as van Mander mentions the panel erroneously under
the works of Orley. The bare, soberly composed picture shows the
Madonna and St. Luke in a magnificent stone prison. Space and cubic
volume are clearly articulated, exact and impeccable. Gossaert's later
works are increasingly dominated by constructive reasoning. If the passion
for rule, measure and theory became a danger even for Dürer, a master
of infinitely greater profundity, how much further away from the sources
of sound design must Gossaert have been led.

In those critical days when tradition had disintegrated in the North,
rationalism was an ever-present menace. The master was pre-occupied
by particular problems of form and particular difficulties. And in working
with arrogant pedantry to produce striking effects of perspective foreshortening and overlappings he loses the spiritual content. What was a
means to an end for a Leonardo da Vinci here became the end in itself.

Gossaert represented *Adam and Eve* several times. He welcomed the
task of depicting nude bodies in life-size. Van Mander mentions one
such work. An original is in the Berlin museum, another at Hampton 211
Court. Copies exist of the second composition, one of them also in Berlin,
another (purchased as an original) in Brussels. A third composition survives in an original drawing in the Albertina, Vienna. A fourth with complicated postures, in bad taste, is at Schloss Schönhausen near Berlin.[3]

Just as Gossaert liked to make his figures as large as possible and
showed little feeling for the irrationalities of the landscape, he favoured
half-length figures for saints set against a neutral background and within
a narrow framework. He depicted St. Donatian—at Tournai—in this
way. On the back of the panel are the arms of Carondelet. I suspect that
with the Carondelet portrait [formerly] belonging to Mr. R. von Gut-
mann, Vienna,[4] it formed a diptych. There is a *St. Mary Magdalen* in half-

---

[*1] Now in the Van Beuningen Collection, Vierhouten.
[*2] Now in the Mauritshuis, The Hague. More recently the portrait has been attributed by
several scholars to 'Master Michiel' (Michiel Sittow).
[*3] Now at Jagdschloss Grunewald, Berlin. On Gossaert's *Adam and Eve* compositions cf. the
detailed study by H. Schwarz, in *Gazette des Beaux-Arts*, series 6, vol. XLII, 1953, pp. 145–82.
[*4] Now in the William Rockhill Gallery of Art, Kansas City, Missouri.

length in the Musée Mayer van den Bergh, Antwerp. A smaller *Magdalen* in half-length which was acquired a few years ago for the National Gallery, London, was certainly done much earlier and fascinates by the individualized naivety of its expression. This panel, despite the not quite perfect condition, takes its rightful place alongside the Palermo triptych. Gossaert's compositional ability fails him when he is called on to produce many-figured scenes. The excessive modelling of the details impairs the rhythm and impact of the whole. All the parts push forward ostentatiously.

The famous altarpiece at Middelburg was destroyed by fire. A *Descent from the Cross*, in my opinion a work by Gossaert, is exhibited as 'Orley' in the Hermitage, St. Petersburg (it came from the collection of King William of Holland).[1] This panel, which was transferred to canvas and has unfortunately lost much of its clarity and precision, may be identical with a picture by Gossaert that van Mander saw in the house of a Mr. Magnus of Haarlem.[2]

215    The master is more successful depicting figures in ceremonial array than with dramatic scenes. His picture of *St. Luke* in the Vienna museum, which differs considerably from the altar panel of the same subject in Prague—perhaps inspired by a borrowed model (Joos van Cleve)—and probably dates from about 1518, is successful in composition.

For some reason or other an *Ecce Homo*, done by Gossaert about 1527, the original of which cannot be traced today, was frequently copied. The copyists (among them the Master of the Female Half-Lengths) generally added the honest inscription *Malbodius invenit*, but often it was *Malbodius pingebat*.

Of the mythological nudities, of which Gossaert was assuredly very proud—when he introduced such subjects he regarded himself as a learned connoisseur of antiquity and an enlightened son of a new age—I

213    have already mentioned the panels in Berlin and in the Cook Collection (1516 and 1517). Similarly conceived individual female nudes, on a smaller scale, are in Rovigo museum and in the Schloss Collection, Paris.[3]

212    The *Danae* in Munich, a carefully executed original of 1527, is sculpturesque in conception and makes a cold, metallic impression.

A large number of *Madonnas*, in particular Madonnas in half-length,

---

[1] In the 1958 Hermitage Catalogue of Western paintings the picture is listed as a work of Gossaert. The wings with *St. John* and *St. Peter* and, on the reverse, the *Annunciation*, have recently come to light again and are now in the Museum of Art, Toledo, Ohio. They are dated 1521.

[2] From documents published by J. Maréchal in *Académie Royale de Belgique, Classe des Beaux-Arts, Memoires*, XIII, No. 2, Brussels, 1963, pp. 11–15, it is now clear that the altarpiece was originally in the Salamanca Chapel of the Augustinian Church at Bruges, where it remained at least until 1795.

[3] Now in the Royal Museum, Brussels.

survive. A few, with complicated postures and skilful drawing enjoyed much popularity and were frequently copied. The emotional coldness, which alienates us, offended no one. Amongst Gossaert's Madonnas is a very fine original which forms one half of the Carondelet triptych in the 219–220 Louvre (1517); of approximately the same date and scarcely inferior in quality is a panel in the E. Simon Collection, Berlin (from the Kaufmann Collection).[1]

An unusual number of mediocre copies, the original of which has not been traced, exist of a pretentious composition in which the Christ Child is attempting to disentangle Himself from His mother's veil. Most of these copies dating from about 1550 are similar in style. Could they have been done by Paulus van Aalst, of whom van Mander states that he was exceptionally good at copying works by Jan van Mabuse? The son of Pieter Coeck could well be responsible for the effeminate style.

Another almost equally popular type is a *Virgin and Child* in which the hair of the Madonna is parted in a striking way. Several good replicas come close to Gossaert, even in the execution, as for instance the panel at Longford Castle and the one formerly in the R. Kann Collection.[2] There is something portrait-like in the appearance of the Mother and the Child and in this connection van Mander's passage has been recalled in which he relates that Gossaert was supposed to have painted the wife and son of his patron, the Marquis de Vere (Adolph of Burgundy), as the Virgin with the Christ Child. The partly accredited portrait of the Marquise (in the Gardner Museum, Boston) does not at any rate preclude this possibility.

An almost forgotten Madonna panel by Gossaert was sold with the Beurnonville Collection and is now in the Max Wassermann Collection, Paris.[3]

The number of portraits is considerable. Clear in form, often with considerable movement in the hands, self-assured in expression, in a narrow frame and often powerfully modelled against a neutral ground, these works are more impressive than the master's free inventions. The modelling is brilliant, achieved not so much by deep shadows as by keenly observed reflexes, and skilful, at times almost exaggerated drawing of intersecting parts and foreshortening. Examples are easy to find in the large galleries, in particular in the National Gallery, London, in the Louvre, in Berlin, Vienna, Antwerp.

*[1] Later in the Huck Collection, Berlin.
*[2] Now in the Metropolitan Museum of Art, New York.
*[3] The collection has been divided among the heirs of Mr. Wassermann.

Gossaert solved the rather unusual problem of a group portrait of
221 children when he painted the three Danish royal children in one panel.
Three versions of this picture, more or less equal in quality, survive in
England—at Hampton Court, Wilton House, and Longford Castle. The
master must also have painted Christian of Denmark, the father of these
children. Jacob Binck's engraved portrait of this king, judging by its
style, is based on Gossaert.[1]

Gossaert was not so closely connected with the Habsburg regent as was
162 his rival Orley but the link with the Danish king, who was married to
Isabella of Austria, is sufficient evidence that Gossaert's services were
appreciated at court. Orley was more readily available and had to replace
(inadequately as we believe) the most capable of the Netherlandish
portrait painters around 1525.

Justi's attempts to trace portraits of members of the Habsburg family by
Gossaert were not successful. Recently I saw a portrait on the Italian art
market[2] that looks like a portrait by our master and seems to represent a
sister of Charles V. The similarity with the best authenticated portrait
of the Danish queen (in the collection of Count Tarnowski) is very striking
—but it could equally well represent her sister Mary of Hungary, whose
known portraits date from a much later period.

Gossaert develops his manner of drawing, in deliberate contrast to
Netherlandish tradition, to a full, rounded breadth of form, a spirited,
undulating ductus with clear and precise demarcations. His highest aim
is to achieve the striking illusion of physical form. Sensitivity, light, air,
material texture, charm of colour—all are sacrificed. Gossaert seeks out
difficulties and emphasizes them. He treats us to amazing aspects, not
justified by the content, merely to be different from the others and to show
off his art. Not infrequently his figures appear rigid in eccentric poses,
because his analytical approach and adherence to the model impede the
flow of movement.

No one could have been worse equipped to convey visions, dreams or
spook. His fanatical devotion to physical form spoilt him as interpreter
of Christian spirituality and in this negative sense he was truly 'modern',
for he only believed what he saw and he only saw what he could actually
touch.

*1 The original drawing by Gossaert has come to light again and is now in the F. Lugt Collec-
tion, Paris. Cf. Friedländer's paper on the portraits of the Danish king (in *Annuaire des Musées
Royaux de Beaux-Arts de Belgique*, I, 1938), where Jacob Binck too is rejected as the engraver,
although there is in fact also an engraved portrait of Christian II by Binck.

*2 Later in the August van Berg Collection, Portland, Oregon.

# JAN JOEST

A SINGLE work, however significant, is not, generally speaking, sufficient to illuminate its author's personality from all sides. Characteristic qualities must recur in other works if our conception of the author is to be confirmed and completed.

Jan Joest is everywhere named in connection with the wings of the Kalkar altarpiece, but since the proposal to identify him with the Master of the Death of the Virgin was—quite rightly—rejected, no further attempt has been made to insert him correctly in the historical chain. In 1904, when the wings were exhibited at Düsseldorf, comment on the isolated altar work was limited to conventional words of praise.

Kalkar documents have supplied us with the information that Jan Joosten carried out the great task of painting the two wings with twenty pictures, five on each side, between 1505 and 1508. As far as we can gather from the payment entries, the painter seems to have come from outside to do the work at Kalkar and to have departed after he had completed his task. On the other hand the painter's name was found in a Kalkar list of soldiers for the year 1480. It was, so one assumes, on the strength of this earlier association with Kalkar that the master received the commission in 1505. Perhaps he was a native of the town. 229

It so happens that the name of a painter, Jan Joest, has been found in a far more celebrated art centre than Kalkar ever was, namely Haarlem. And the identification of the Haarlem artist with the Kalkar one has been everywhere accepted.

In 1510, i.e. after the years at Kalkar, Jan Joest purchased a house in the Dutch town;[1] in 1515 he executed a commission for the church of St. Bavo; in 1519 he was buried in that church. The Haarlem and the Kalkar dates agree. But prior to 1505 there is no trace of Jan Joest at Haarlem. From which town he had come to Kalkar must remain an open question.[2]

There is an altarpiece in the cathedral of Palencia to which, as to so many noteworthy monuments in Spain, C. Justi has drawn attention.[3] In the church records the painter's name is given as Juan de Holanda.

[1] In 1512 he painted the high altar of the abbey church of St. Ludger at Werden (J. H. Schmidt, *Kalkar*, 1950, p. 63).
[2] Friedländer (*Die Altniederländische Malerei*, XIV, 1937, p. 114) thinks it probable that Joest was born at Wesel, as according to a newly-found document he was in that town as early as 1474.
[3] *Miszellaneen aus drei Jahrhunderten Spanischen Kunstlebens*, I, p. 329.

Justi, who describes the altarpiece, raises the question of the identity of this Dutch Jan, he suggests Jan Mostaert. But Jan Mostaert, whose art is now familiar to us, no longer comes into the picture. For anyone who has seen the Kalkar altar wings one glance at the Palencia panels is sufficient to reveal the similarity of style. And even those who do not trust this impression will be forced to admit that the probabilities are all in favour of the identification.

Jan Joosten of Kalkar is probably none other than Jan Joest of Haarlem; the name Juan de Holanda would therefore be applicable to him. That a Jan of Holland should have produced work at Palencia related in style to the Kalkar altar wings and not be identical with Jan Joest is all the more improbable because relations between Spain and Holland were comparatively rare. The identification provides welcome confirmation of the Kalkar records and of the connection between the Kalkar and the Haarlem records.

225–227 The altarpiece at Palencia—always according to Justi—was 'commissioned in 1505 in Brussels' by Juan de Fonseca. Strangely enough the commissions for Kalkar and Palencia came at the same time. This gives rise to difficulties, but they are not by any means insuperable. Before he went to Kalkar Jan Joest could have been living in Brussels or he could have been called to Brussels to receive the commission from the Spaniard, who was there on a diplomatic mission. If the inscription, which I am unable to check, really reads 'Commissioned 1505' it is not easy to believe that Jan Joest before he went to Kalkar found time to execute the commission. And the idea that he worked at the Palencia panels during his years at Kalkar is an awkward one. Perhaps he postponed the execution of the work until after the Kalkar period. Or perhaps the inscription means that the altarpiece was completed in 1505 and would thus have been finished before the Kalkar work. Incidentally in Justi's introduction to the Baedeker of Spain the date of the altarpiece is given as 1507.

Only a calculating scholar, but never an unbiassed observer, could be reminded of Geertgen when looking at the Kalkar wings. The Haarlem tradition, the continuing effects of Geertgen's influence, are apparent in the work of Jan Mostaert but not in that of Jan Joest. The stylistic phase is a different one, the source of this art is not known—which is not surprising considering the scarcity of surviving Dutch monuments of the fifteenth century. But this does not entitle us to regard the master as an original genius. Nevertheless Jan Joest is well to the fore amongst the painters who are looking for new ideas. We are at the beginning of the sixteenth century but the nearest stylistic parallel is to be found in the work of Joos van Cleve, who became master at Antwerp in 1511, and in the earliest works of Barthel Bruyn, who was only twelve years old in 1505. Eisenmann in particular emphasized the affinity with the Master of the Death of the Virgin and he was even tempted to amalgamate the two artists; the relationship to Bruyn was cleverly detected by Firmenich-Richartz.

We are approximately in the artistic phase of Hans Holbein the elder, but the broader, more painterly approach of the Netherlandish artist contrasts with the more linear style of the South German master. What they have in common is the easy unconcern with which they loosen the ties of traditional stylistic severity, the abrupt juxtaposition of realistic portrait-like heads and empty, mask-like ideal heads. The impulse to express powerful movement fizzles out without producing a more dramatically intensified composition. The construction of the figures is uncertain although the succulent, glowing colour, the sense of reality in the rendering of unimportant details and the charm of changing effects of light successfully conceal the innate weakness.

The conception is comfortably bourgeois, at times even humorous, rather than dignified or representative in the spirit of the Church. Comical 'nursery' motifs and caricature, which are introduced wherever opportunity arises, supply evidence enough that for this ancestor of Dutch portrait, landscape and genre painting religious painting was an uncongenial task to which he had perforce to resign himself.

The badly foreshortened figures of the Apostles with their stuck-on beards are just as unconvincing as the tender-hearted figure of Our Lord, whereas the incidental figures, with eyes slit open and strongly sensuous mouths, are striking in their individual realism. The hands are conspicuously large with long, bony, flexible fingers. The children, women and youthful men often have upturned noses which produces a comic, impudent or vulgar impression.

The Palencia picture is divided in an unusual way into eight panels, eight representations, with three each on the right and on the left, two in the centre one above the other. The main panel, the lower central one, is twice as large as the others both in size and in the scale of the figures. The scenes are separated by a powerfully moulded Gothic framework. The dominant composition in the centre, a group of St. John the Evangelist standing at the back of and supporting the mourning figure of 225 the kneeling Virgin, shows a simplicity, nobility and tenderness beyond anything achieved in the Kalkar work. To the right kneels the donor

Juan de Fonseca. The smaller panels from the top left downwards represent:

  1. *The young Jesus disputing in the Temple.* An interior with bold perspective construction, consistent treatment of the lighting, surprising chiaroscuro.

226  2. *The Flight into Egypt.*

  3. *The Presentation in the Temple.* This scene is also represented in the Kalkar altar work.

  4. (Top centre) *Christ carrying the Cross.*

  5. (Top right) *The Crucifixion.*

  6. *The Lamentation over Christ.*

227  7. *The Entombment.*

Judging by the style, the Palencia altarpiece seems a little older than the Kalkar work. I am therefore inclined to believe that it was completed in 1505, before Jan Joest went to Kalkar. The composition in the great majority of the Palencia panels is calmer, less diffuse than in the Kalkar ones, the types are more dignified, the execution more uniform.

There is at Sigmaringen a painting by Jan Joest, stylistically close to the Palencia altarpiece, which is strikingly original in composition—a

228 *Lamentation over Christ.*[1] In the centre is the Virgin Mary with the Body of Christ, holding her Son in the manner of God the Father in early representations of the Trinity, to the left St. John supporting the weight, to the right the Magdalen holding the left arm of the Saviour. The scene appears soft and painterly against a dark landscape in the middle ground. Under No. 72 (formerly Weyer Collection 149) of the Sigmaringen catalogue the picture is described, on Scheibler's and Eisenmann's authority, as an early work by Bruyn.

We find a clue that leads to Jan Joest in the von Kaufmann Collection, Berlin. This collection once included the well-known Bruyn panel dated 1516, a *Nativity* with brilliantly executed lighting.[2] A comparison with the *Nativity* at Kalkar, where the kneeling figure of the Virgin is similarly shown, reveals that in 1516 Bruyn (he was then 24 years old) was slavishly dependent on Jan Joest.

Bruyn's composition is derivative. It is also to be found elsewhere. There was a second *Nativity* in the von Kaufmann Collection, rather inferior in execution, which has nothing whatever to do with Bruyn but repeats all essential motifs of the Bruyn panel, in particular the group

*[1] Now in the Wallraf-Richartz Museum, Cologne.
*[2] Now in the Staedel Institute, Frankfurt.

of kneeling angels standing head to head behind and a little to the side of the crib. I am convinced from stylistic grounds that the two versions go back to a picture by Jan Joest that can no longer be traced today. In 1508, when Jan Joest left Kalkar probably proceeding direct to Haarlem (he was certainly in Haarlem by 1510), Barthel Bruyn was only fifteen years of age. He was most likely trained in the Dutch town between 1510 and 1515. The name Bruyn occurs in 1490 on a Haarlem document. The painter Bruyn who worked there for the church of St. Bavo in 1490 may have been Barthel's father.

In the museum at Valenciennes there is a panel with a fairly exact copy by the so-called Master of Frankfurt of the picture we know from 231 the von Kaufmann Collection.[1] The Master of Frankfurt was older than Bruyn, and was probably active at Antwerp as early as 1500. His lack of independence and his tendency to borrow compositions can be observed also in other cases. Without having been actually a pupil of Jan Joest he may have made use of the model. It is not by any means out of the question that Jan Joest, directly or indirectly, exerted an influence on the Southern Netherlands. For was he not, if the Palencia inscription is genuine, in Brussels in 1505?

Joos van Cleve has been confused with Jan Joest and the stylistic affinity between the Cleve master and Bruyn has been emphasized repeatedly. The relationship can best be sorted out by assuming that Bruyn and Joos van Cleve were pupils of Jan Joest and regarding what they had in common as derived from the common teacher. Joos was a little older than Bruyn. He begins as Master in 1511 but may have started to work a few years earlier, perhaps in 1507; Bruyn did not begin until 1515. Joos, always provided he really did work in Jan Joest's workshop, may well have been at Kalkar around 1506. This connection is not improbable, considering how close Cleve is to Kalkar.

There is in the von Bissing Collection, Munich, a small *Nativity* which, without being a replica of the model we have reconstructed, has many features in common with it, e.g. the hands of the Virgin and the position of the Child; in quality it far surpasses any of the panels compared here including the ones by Bruyn and the Frankfurt master. This panel is certainly an original, in my opinion it could well be an original by Jan Joest. The well-preserved parts, in particular the flying angels at the top, are quite masterly. The heads of St. Joseph and of the Virgin are not in perfect condition and probably for that reason seem a little strange.

Jan's art, the force of which has not been properly appreciated, had

[1] Exhibited Paris 1904, Exposition des Primitifs Français, No. 115, Photo Giraudon.

manifold and wide repercussions. The centre probably lay within the boundaries of Holland even though the master's origins are obscure. The influence of Jan, who worked at Kalkar, perhaps in Brussels, at Haarlem and for Palencia, spread to Antwerp (Master of Frankfurt, Joos van Cleve) and to Cologne (Barthel Bruyn).

The threads that bind his art to the older Dutch art are not visible. But if we are ever bold enough to attempt a reconstruction of the evolution of Dutch art, of the growth of the characteristics which in the seventeenth century emerge so triumphantly as specifically Dutch, then Jan Joest will find his place as an essential link between Geertgen and Jan van Scorel.

# JAN MOSTAERT

IN as far as we rely on van Mander's account we enjoy the advantage of a fairly informative biography of Jan Mostaert. It was at Haarlem in particular that van Mander pursued his investigations with such zeal, where in many of the houses he was shown pictures by 'old Masters' and where he came upon a living tradition relating to Mostaert. As long as that painter's activity remained attached to Haarlem, van Mander's account is reliable. In his Life of Ouwater van Mander refers to an honest old man, the painter Aelbert Simonsz, who in 1604 claimed to have been, some sixty years previously, that is in 1544, a pupil of Jan Mostaert at the time about seventy years of age. In his biography of Mostaert van Mander says that the painter died at a ripe old age about 1555 or 1556. Two documents published by Van der Willigen,[1] which have been much neglected of late, confirm these dates. As early as 1500 Mostaert received a commission for a painting at Haarlem, which means that at that time he was already working there as master.[2] He left the city 'where he had been living until then' at an advanced age. Probably most of van Mander's information came from the lips of Mostaert's pupil Simonsz—that is from a good source. In his valuable contribution to the life of Geertgen, this witness makes the assertion that Mostaert (although he was born as early as c. 1475[3]) never met Geertgen, from which we can deduce that he would certainly have known Geertgen if the latter had lived long enough. It would thus seem that not only was Mostaert born in Haarlem, not only did he live and teach there towards the end of his life (about 1546) but he was also trained there. He must therefore have been closely linked to the Haarlem art tradition. This is supported by the information that when still very young he was a pupil of Jacob of Haarlem, who executed the 'Zakkedragers' (corn carriers) altarpiece for the great church there. We have no further information about this Jacob[4] unless we venture to assume

[1] *Les Artistes de Haarlem* (1870).
[2] Mostaert is mentioned as a painter in Haarlem records as early as 1498 (see Thierry de Bye Dolleman, in *Jaarboek voor het Centraal Bureau voor Genealogie*, XVII, 1963, pp. 1 ff.).
[3] Thanks to the research of M. Thierry de Bye Dolleman, loc. cit, we can now give the date of Mostaert's birth more precisely as c. 1472/1473.
[4] Jacob of Haarlem has been tentatively identified with the so-called Master of the Brunswick Diptych (cf. p. 53, note 3), a follower of Geertgen (see Exhibition catalogue *Middeleeuwse Kunst der Noordelijke Nederlanden*, Amsterdam, 1958, pp. 55 f.).

that he is identical with an anonymous painter who stands, stylistically, between Geertgen and Mostaert.

Van Mander speaks very highly of the refined habits and the courtesy of Mostaert who, he says, was the descendant of an old and noble family. A period of activity at court interrupts like an episode the long years of his Haarlem activity.[1] For eighteen years, so van Mander maintains, probably on information received from old Simonsz, Mostaert was painter to the Regent Margaret, staying wherever that regent held her court. Unfortunately no documentary confirmation for this report has been forthcoming and the master's name does not occur on any of the lists of pictures belonging to Margaret. The daughter of the emperor Maximilian was regent of the Netherlands from 1506 to 1529 (the year of her death). Van Orley was her court painter between 1518 and 1529, Jacopo de' Barbari between 1510 and 1515. The only document from the court that seems to refer to Mostaert is somewhat obscure. A payment was made in 1521 '*a ung painctre qui a présenté a Madame une paincture de feu Notre Seigneur de Savoye faict en vif, nommé Jehan Masturd: XX philippus*'. The man portrayed can only be Philibert of Savoy, Margaret's husband, who had died before 1504. If we are to take the text literally it would mean that prior to 1504, when he was still very young, Mostaert had been in contact with Margaret's husband. The fact that seventeen years after the death of Philibert he should sell to that prince's widow a portrait of the prince painted from life is hard to explain and scarcely tallies with the information that he had been eighteen years in her service.

Van Mander describes a whole series of works by Mostaert that he had seen at Haarlem and The Hague. The majority was shown to him in the house of Niclaes Suyker, Mayor of Haarlem. Suyker was a grandson of Mostaert and, one presumes, was able to give accurate accounts of his ancestor and to confirm or supplement Simonsz's statements.

Art critics have succeeded in reconstructing step by step the work of a master whose identity with Jan Mostaert, first advocated by G. Glück, became more and more apparent the more pictures came to light. There are many passages by van Mander that apply to the work of this painter who, once his personality began to take shape, became known as the 'Master of the Herald'. In the work of this anonymous master we come upon a link with Haarlem: in rather an inferior triptych, namely, which at least follows his style, Geertgen's Haarlem *Lamentation of Christ* is copied.

---

*[1] The earliest record of Jan Mostaert's connection with Haarlem is a recently discovered document referring to the purchase by him of half a house in Haarlem in 1498 (see catalogue of the exhibition *Le Siècle de Bruegel*, Brussels, 1963, p. 163).

Distinguished personalities, who according to van Mander were anxious to have their portraits painted by Margaret's court painter, are not infrequently seen in the reconstructed *oeuvre*. We find members of leading Dutch families, the Alkemades, the Bronckhorsts, and the Wassenaers. The *Portrait of a Lady* in the Würzburg museum represents 233, 235 Justina van Wassenaer—as Grete Ring has shown.[1] The portrait of the lady's husband, Jan van Wassenaer, survives in copies at least. Courtly, ceremonial dignity is characteristic for all portraits by the presumptive Mostaert.

Van Mander mentions among Mostaert's pictures in the house of the Haarlem Mayor a portrait of the countess Jacobaea. The lady in question is Jacqueline of Bavaria, who was ruler of Holland, not, as might be expected, in Mostaert's day but a century earlier. The master copied an older portrait, probably for a Dutch town hall where the display of a series of portraits of the lords of the land was intended. We are familiar with Jacqueline's features not only from a copy in the Portrait Codex of Arras but from what is probably an original drawing in Frankfurt and which we can tentatively attribute to Jan van Eyck. In the gallery of Copenhagen there is a painting of this royal lady which is close in style to the works of the presumptive Jan Mostaert.

Furthermore: the strangest item in van Mander's list of pictures can be traced in the *oeuvre* of our master, namely 'a West Indian landscape with many nude people, a fantastic cliff and exotic houses and huts'. In a 241 Dutch private collection E. Weiss[2] found a picture that would fit this description and it reveals the style that we have ample grounds for regarding as the style of Jan Mostaert. The surviving picture[3] may not be identical with the one van Mander saw and which he considered unfinished but just as it is quite conceivable that Jan Mostaert painted more than one West Indian landscape so it is unlikely that round about 1520 anyone else should have hit upon such an unusual subject. A self-portrait of Jan Mostaert is described in detail by van Mander. A distinguishing feature, an unusual addition, are the small figures in the background: Christ as Judge in the Heavens, the painter as a nude kneeling figure, a devil with the book of sins and an interceding angel. Neither this self-portrait nor indeed any other portrait with such secondary motifs has been found, but the custom of enlivening the background landscapes of the portraits, especially the skies, with small but significant figures is a

---

[1] *Repertorium f. Kunstwissenschaft*, XXXIII, p. 418.
[2] *Zeitschrift f. bildende Kunst* 1909/10, p. 215.
*[3] Now in the Frans Hals Museum, Haarlem.

striking characteristic of our master. The most popular of these narrative additions was the representation of the sibyl pointing out the visionary figure of the Madonna in the heavens to the emperor Augustus. This background scene occurs in the portrait of an elderly bald-headed gentleman in the Copenhagen gallery, in the portrait of a man in the Brussels gallery, in which a whole assortment of little figures and animals has been added, and in a rather rubbed portrait of a woman in the depot of the Berlin museum. A scene from the legend of St. Hubert has been inserted in the

234 landscape in the *Portrait of a Young Man* in the Liverpool gallery.

Jan Mostaert worked for many decades with unvarying conscientiousness. Between 1500 and 1553 he passed through changing phases of taste but deep down he remained untouched by new demands. At bottom his variegated colour and hesitant manner remained at the level of 1500. A comparison in particular with Jacob Cornelisz of Amsterdam or with the two Leyden painters Engelbrechtsen and Lucas van Leyden reveals his basic conservatism.

Consideration for the wishes of noble patrons, who demanded neat, exact and complete rendering of the costume details and accurate heraldry, lends a trivial, pedantic touch to his work. Whilst his contemporaries in Leyden and Amsterdam considered themselves progressive with their use of a vigorous impasto or broad blot-like technique, Jan Mostaert held fast to a careful smooth execution and never sacrificed local colours in the interests of harmony or chiaroscuro, or to achieve in his compositions a fully co-ordinate whole.

The master's chief work, the triptych with the *Descent from the Cross* in

237 the central panel, executed for the Haarlem juror Albert von Adrichem, which passed from the d'Oultremont Collection to the Brussels gallery, though a staggering achievement, reveals his poverty of spirit far more obviously than do the more modest works, and for all its magnificence and for all its ostentation it remains painfully dull and empty. In the composition of the central panel the master's inability to escape the memory of Rogier's Escorial panel, which he knew either in the original or from one of the many imitations, provokes a most dangerous comparison. The overall solemnity of effect is lacking. The eye seeks for a point of anchorage in the even, monotonous daylight, in the dense proximity of compositionally equal figures and is everywhere held up by the irritating virtuosity of the realism in trivial details, especially in the materials. Nevertheless Mostaert's perseverance and conscientiousness bring about a veritable *tour de force*. If, as I cannot help suspecting, in this his main work the master was striving to compete with Quentin Massys to

emulate not only his compositional principles but also his conception, then we must note that he replaced the deep emotional pathos with an at times indifferent, at times over-sweet emotionalism and instead of the solemn melodious flow of Quentin's drapery produced a monotonous, weak undulation.

The master's manner of treating materials, avoiding all sharp angularity, and using schematic, sinuous lines is ever his most salient feature. His large, empty, globular 'lathe-turned' male heads with low receding foreheads and shallow-set eyes are represented full face or in profile. Attempts at foreshortening are unsuccessful. In expressing dignity he never quite avoids a 'bigwig' pomposity.

Mostaert's unsubstantial and rather exquisite art is better suited to the smaller panel in which he can excel with neat precision and has no need to puff up his talent. The dainty little *Adoration of the Kings* in the Rijks- 239 museum, Amsterdam, is an enchanting example. Such pictures with their multiple divisions and fine articulation are gay and animated in effect. In the National Gallery, London, there is a very small and therefore little noticed work by Mostaert, a *Head of St. John the Baptist with Angels*, which positively sparkles.

A prevailing weakness in the execution of the torso, with long limbs to which are attached hands with shrivelled palms and comparatively long fingers, is a characteristic feature of the master's style. A thin, feathery vegetation almost invariably covers the mountains and ruins in the landscape backgrounds that are always heavily charged with over-minutely executed details. The foliage of the trees in the middle-ground often appears spherically shaped. A comparison with contemporaries such as Orley or Lucas van Leyden would entitle us to expect in Mostaert's production which lasted over a period of six decades, changes so fundamental as to make a link between beginning and end almost imperceptible. Whilst the fairly long sequence of known works by Mostaert may reach neither to the beginning nor to the end, it almost certainly covers a long period of time. We may attempt a rough chronological classification of the pictures but nowhere do we find any changes of direction. The uniformity of style remains essentially intact.

The panel with the *Tree of Jesse* (Stroganoff Collection, Rome, $22\frac{7}{8} \times$ 240 $34\frac{1}{4}$ in.)[1] is the most archaic work that I feel justified in attributing to Mostaert. This panel may date from c. 1500. It is decorative in design,

[1] Illustrated, amongst others, in Dülberg, *Frühholländer in Italien*, with the attribution 'School of Geertgen'. *Now in the Rijksmuseum, Amsterdam, where the painting is ascribed to Geertgen. This attribution, accepted by several scholars, has recently been rejected by K. G. Boon (in *Oud-Holland*, LXXXI, 1966, pp. 61 ff.), who supports Friedländer's view with cogent arguments.

iridescent and truly dazzling in the foppish costume display. The echo of Geertgen is not surprising.

The Alkemade triptych may have originated about a decade later. It is now in the Provinzialmuseum, Bonn (formerly Wesendonck Collection; Düsseldorf Exhibition, 1904, Pl. 59).

To judge from the costumes, several portraits may be dated about 1520. The portrait of Jan van Wassenaer in the Louvre (or at any rate the original) must have been done between 1516 and 1523.

A small panel with *Christ before Pilate*, not mentioned anywhere, passed from the Collection of Sir John Ramsden to the London art market.[1]

Another—hitherto unknown—slightly later picture by the Master, an *Ecce Homo*, is at Northwick Park.[2]

The large many-figured *Crucifixion*, a busy turbulent scene, in the Johnson Collection, Philadelphia, also came from the Northwick Park Collection, which formerly contained many more Early Netherlandish rarities than it does today. I am inclined to regard this work as rather late, circa 1530. The comparatively free and asymmetrical arrangement, the deliberate attempt at dramatic effect, the gradation in the scale of the figures which produces an unexpected feeling of depth, all this suggests a later date of origin. Massys's influence, so predominant in the Oultremont altarpiece, is no longer perceptible.

I regard as one of the later works the large *Landscape with St. Christopher* in the Musée Mayer van den Bergh, Antwerp, a picture that may be identical with a work van Mander saw in the house of Jan Claesz at The Hague and which he describes as follows: 'a St. Christopher in a landscape, a large picture.' In the construction of the landscape the master seems to stand about half-way between Patenier and Pieter Bruegel. The clumsy head of the saint is not successful in the foreshortening.

A few works that we can attribute to our master on stylistic grounds bring us at least close to the court of the Habsburg regent. There is a portrait of a man in the Prado[3] which, though perhaps only a copy, does show characteristic features of Mostaert's style, particularly in the lines of the drapery and in the landscape motifs. And this portrait represents Philibert of Savoy, Margaret's husband who died prematurely. The costume, it is true, which seems to fit a period around 1520 rather than 1504, raises an awkward problem.

An apparently delicately executed portrait in the Mostaert style, known to me only from the photogravure in the catalogue of the Lepke

*[1] Later in the G. Tillmann Collection, Amsterdam.
*[2] Sold in 1965 after the death of Captain E. G. Spencer Churchill.
*[3] Now in the Museo de Santa Cruz, Toledo.

sale (12 Dec. 1888 No. 51, 'Holbein') seems to represent King Ferdinand, Margaret's nephew, as a youth of 20 years. The likeness is by no means striking.

Finally an echo of Mostaert's style can be found in an altar panel in the Copenhagen museum, which was donated by Christian II of Denmark and his wife Isabel (circa 1518). And Isabel was Margaret's niece.[1]

The Copenhagen panel is similar in arrangement and in the compositional idea to the Alkemade triptych. The royal donors in front take up the entire width of the picture whilst the traditional figures of the Last Judgement—Christ as Judge, St. Michael, the elect and the damned—though less accessory-like than in the altarpiece in the von Wesendonck Collection, are certainly of little consequence and seem to have been given makeshift accommodation.

It was Grete Ring who succeeded in proving that a picture fully described in the inventory of the regent's art collections, but without artist's name, was a work by Mostaert.[2] The description fits a *Christis as Man of Sorrows* in the Museo Civico, Verona, a picture that I had attributed to our painter many years ago. There was a replica of equal quality in the S. Wedells Collection, Hamburg[3] (formerly belonging to M. Colnaghi, London) which like the version in Verona could be identical with the work formerly belonging to Margaret.

238

In addition to these representations of the suffering Redeemer in half-length with a ring of angels on a red ground, Jan Mostaert also represented several times the rather plaintive *Man of Sorrows* without the characteristic addition of small figures. To the version in the Willett Collection that was in Bruges in 1902 (No. 338, photo Bruckmann[4]), I can add one with only slight differences in composition, in the Provincial Museum in Burgos. A third was once in the Lanfranconi Collection (Sale 1895, No. 46), a fourth belonged to Mr. von Stolk, The Hague, a fifth has recently appeared on the Amsterdam art market.

Compositions with life-size figures did not seem to occur in the *oeuvre* of the master. Formerly this rather disturbed me because van Mander mentions two works with half-length figures in life-size, and in view of the master's obvious preference for small figures I could not quite believe that he would have attempted them.

Recently, however, I saw a panel by Mostaert—which turned up on

---

*[1] According to E. Moltke (in *Nationalmuseets Arbejdsmarkt*, 1955, pp. 87 f.) the Copenhagen painting, which has also been attributed to Jacob Cornelisz van Oostsanen, was produced before March 1515.
  [2] *Monatshefte für Kunstwissenschaft*, VII, 1914.    *[3] Now in the Kunsthalle, Hamburg.
  *[4] Now in the National Gallery, London.

the London art market—with half-length figures in life-size, that actually corresponds in subject-matter to a work mentioned by van Mander, namely an *Ecce Homo*—in not quite perfect condition. Unfortunately it is by no means identical with the picture described. At any rate the myrmidon who holds Christ has no 'plastered' head.

236    Dr. Oertel's Collection in Munich contains a fairly large panel by our master with full-length figures of *Abraham and Hagar*, in half-size.[1] This subject, too, is mentioned in van Mander's list but the pictures cannot be identical because van Mander speaks of half-lengths.

Even though the text of the Haarlem document stating that Mostaert left his native town, where he had been living until then, at an advanced age seems to indicate that his art, purely Dutch, grew and thrived on Haarlem soil, yet the character of his art refutes this and confirms van Mander's information that he worked for the court in the West.

242–245    In comparison to Cornelis Engelbrechtsen and Jacob Cornelisz, approximately contemporary Dutch artists, Mostaert seems less robust and less bourgeois, and exacting aristocratic standards appreciably modified his style. We can accept Mostaert as follower and pupil in the second generation of Geertgen but never as his direct successor.

*[1] Now in the Schloss Rohoncz Collection (Baron Thyssen), Lugano-Castagnola.

# LUCAS VAN LEYDEN

THE name Lucas van Leyden has an authoritative ring but evokes no specific idea in our minds. He enjoys full and genuine popularity only with collectors and connoisseurs of engravings, who value very highly the precious prints, good impressions of which are rare. Everywhere, especially in Italy, paintings wrongly attributed to him sully his name and confuse our conception of his art. And where indeed could a painting be found with sufficiently salient features and sharply enough defined in character to be capable of upholding his honour! A long uninterrupted sequence of engravings authenticated by signatures and often inscribed with the date reveal the draughtsman. If, armed with this knowledge, the critic then cautiously approaches the paintings, van Mander's account will come to his aid.

Carel van Mander, who around 1600 collected with honest enthusiasm the material for his unfortunately rather meagre *Lives of the Painters*, waxes almost eloquent when he comes to speak of Lucas. In his desire to do justice to the memory of the esteemed engraver he made eager and successful enquiries from the descendants of the master at Leyden, and, we may take it, picked up every scrap of the available tradition.

Lucas, so van Mander tells us, was born in 1494 as the son of the able painter Huig Jacobsz, from whom he received his first instruction. He had a weak constitution, was small in stature and from early boyhood on tireless in his devotion to art. He worked in his native town until his premature end. The biographer knows of only one journey that his hero made, through the Netherlands in 1527 in the company of Jan Gossaert.[1] From Dürer's Diary of his Netherlandish journey we know that Lucas was in Antwerp in 1521. The Dutch painter died as early as 1533.

Among the engravings an important print, *Mohammed and the Monk Sergius*, is dated 1508. Lucas van Leyden was in his fifteenth year when he did this engraving, which is in some respects a full achievement and was not surpassed by subsequent works. The precocity is so extraordinary and unusual that it has served over and again as a basis for an attack against the traditional date of his birth. But all attempts to upset the date have

246

---

*[1] Van Mander does not give the actual date of the journey. He only says that Lucas made the journey when he was 33. This has to be kept in mind in view of the controversy over the year of Lucas's birth (see p. 122, note 1).

proved futile. If van Mander says that Lucas was born in 1494 at the end
of May or the beginning of June then the careful accuracy testifies to the
exactness of the information. Everthing else that he tells us in his account
is, as far as we can check it, accurate. What we know of the circumstances
of the master's life, apart from van Mander's vita—and it is little enough
—confirms his statements. The unusually early maturity of the engraver
was admired as a miracle in the circles from which van Mander drew his
knowledge and the narrator cannot sufficiently extol the deeds of the
infant prodigy. However strongly experience recoils from the idea, we
must for better or for worse accept the date and fit the abnormality into
the picture that we are building of our master.[1]

It would seem, moreover, that the print of 1508 is not even the oldest
of the engravings; there are several undated works, such as the print of the
*Raising of Lazarus*, which are probably even earlier. Admittedly we are
assuming that the young master, still in his boyhood, made exceptionally
rapid progress and that it was a matter not of years but of months or even
weeks for him to wipe out mistakes and to overcome imperfections. His
father was allegedly a painter and no more of an engraver than was
Cornelis Engelbrechtsen, who is mentioned as second teacher. It has not
been possible to bridge the gap between Netherlandish engravers around
1500, about whom we know very little, and the highly developed early
works by Lucas, and it is hardly likely that it ever will be possible. In all
probability the appearance as it were out of the blue of the engraver
Lucas is due to more than a mere gap in our knowledge: he was a genius
even if only on the technical side. We can now proceed to examine the
engravings in the order in which they were produced with the comfortable
knowledge that we have reliable documentary evidence of his development, and trust that despite all changes the master's individuality will
ultimately be revealed. But a spectacle of organic growth is unfortunately
not for us. The path he pursues runs at sixes and sevens, now towards one
goal now towards another and by no means always upwards. The master
does not seem to be surely guided by his personal power of design but
rather to seek models in nature and in the art of others which like
will-o'-the-wisps seem to determine the zig-zag course of the distracted
draughtsman.

Tradition afforded just as little support for Lucas as for his contemporaries. In this dangerous crisis of art the Dutch artist seeks salvation in

---

*1 Despite the attempt by E. Pelinck (in *Oud-Holland*, LXIV, 1949, pp. 193 ff.) to move the
date of birth back to 1489 and to show that van Mander's date 1494 may have been due to a
misunderstanding, Friedländer in *Lucas van Leyden* (edited by F. Winkler and published posthum-
ously in 1963) still favours 1494 as the year of Lucas's birth.

the natural world. From the inexhaustible wealth of nature he enriches his art precipitately, superficially, startlingly, but not consistently, accumulating rather than constructing.

The engraver's ambition, his urge to conquer new ground for the burin, seems positively insatiable. Ever new problems arise, are solved and, apparently, cast aside. As a result of the craftsman's dangerously unlimited skill as an engraver, effort, success and satiety are almost simultaneous.

In the print of 1508 the scene from Mohammed's life is depicted with   246 ingenuously drastic gestures, postures and movements. The prophet has fallen asleep as he sits, the murdered monk lies on the ground, seen in powerful foreshortening, the soldier slips noiselessly between the dead and the sleeping man, exchanging his bloody sword for the clean one of the prophet. The figures are successfully combined in a group. Behind lies a deep hilly landscape the aerial perspective of which is surprisingly well expressed considering the rigidity of the burin. There is no lack of other prints to share in this achievement. But—and this is the astonishing part—Lucas never made further progress along these lines. In not a few of the earliest scenes the spatial depth is exploited to accommodate an animated countryside with bold foreshortenings, compact groupings and a rich variety of landscape elements. Under the assured hand of this engraver the burin runs easily and smoothly acquires the ability to conjure up soft and delicate tones, air and light and a silvery sheen. Despite the amazing mastery of these early prints, round about 1510 Lucas did engravings which apparently show no interest in foreshortening, grouping, spatial depth or dense and delicate strokes, in which the figures seem extraordinarily stiff and stand awkwardly side by side and the view of the landscape is obstructed.

With the famous large *Ecce Homo* of 1510 Lucas achieves his greatest   248 triumph in the rendering of architecture. The wide market-place of complicated shape surrounded by a great variety of buildings, is represented in impeccable perspective and with brilliant clarity of design. Once again the novelty seems to have inspired the master. Christ, shown to the people who are in front of the tribune, is himself indistinctly seen in the middle ground. The gesticulating multitudes fill the wide space in front, and seem, not inaptly, to hold the centre of the stage. But Lucas, as we can also observe elsewhere, did not always follow the content of the narrative but allowed himself to be diverted by thirst for novelty and interest in genre motifs. He enjoyed filling the stage with all kinds of people and in the place of the oft-enacted scene he presented a seemingly new form of rich spectacle.

For the Dutch master the Bible was more a book of stories than an edifying work. At least he took pleasure in drawing inspiration for his art from the anecdotic content of the biblical tale, and his love of spinning **247** yarns often led him to the Old Testament, which had formerly been very rarely drawn upon and then only in relationship to the New. The remoteness and exotic nature of the adventures narrated are expressed superficially and naively by grotesque costume. The Passion series, whilst retaining their traditional spiritual content, were to be transformed from within and inspired with new life. The two series by Lucas that have come down to us are among his most feeble productions. In the earlier one, with the compositions in the round, the master seeks to stimulate interest by a rather clumsy brutality, in the later one he follows Dürer closely, thereby challenging a comparison that goes against him.

A few idyllic prints of his early period, in particular some *Madonnas*, seem permeated by a weary melancholy shown rather awkwardly in the inclination of the head and in the expression of the face. The charm of mood disappears in the course of his further development and is not replaced by a clearer or more differentiated interpretation of spiritual emotion. Altogether Lucas is more physiognomist than a psychologist. He fashions a whole gallery of unusual male heads with over-steep profile lines, projecting chins, curiously modelled noses. The large *Adoration of the Kings* seems to be built around such character heads. At times the rather caricature-like representation goes straight to the heart of the subject as in the print in which David, a robust youth, plays his harp for a rather moody Saul. The accessory figures are generally interesting but the heroes if not exactly devoid of nobility are at least indifferent.

Rooted in a bourgeois milieu, serving neither court nor church, seeking out oddities in everyday life, Lucas also had a natural interest in the wide and diffuse field that we call genre. There can be no doubt that he was in the forefront of the precursors and innovators in this field, not so much because in several prints and in two or three paintings he created the incunabula for this category but rather because his whole narrative is interwoven with genre features and genre motifs.

The master's formal language is in a perpetual state of flux. The figures in his early period are haggard with angular limbs and blunt extremities. Later they tend to be round with swelling contours. The movement, at first rather stilted and hesitant, gradually acquires a greater freedom.

Lucas died young, but from the point of view of what he achieved not prematurely. His later works draw less from the observation of nature than do his early ones.

If around 1520 even Dürer's art had not been without danger for him, around 1530 Marcantonio's manner was to prove disastrous. The Dutch master, who had previously ever preferred the unexpected to the norm, who, if he lacked any talent, lacked a sense of beauty, was bound more inevitably than the majority of his contemporaries to be led astray when he followed the lure of the Southern ideals of form. Northern art was the victim of an extraordinary fatality: the same Marcantonio who had once copied Dürer and had borrowed a landscape motif from a print by Lucas van Leyden, who had certainly been disturbed by the matchless skill of the Dutch engraver, finally emerged as victor, if not thanks to his own ability then at least as representative of a great power advancing to the North—the art of Raphael.

Most of Lucas's paintings are undated. In spite of this we are able to link the pictures historically by comparing them with the unbroken chain of engravings. More than one picture, it is true, perished in the iconoclastic storms, but our stock is far greater than the compilatory literature would lead us to suspect, and is quite sufficient to give a clear idea of the master's manner of painting—once all false attributions have been carefully removed.

The painter does not emerge with the early maturity of the engraver. The paintings that must be regarded as the earliest, such as the *Game of Chess* in the Berlin museum, the slightly later *Beheading of John the Baptist* 251 in the Johnson Collection, Philadelphia, are laboriously painted with intractable colours and multiple brush strokes and seem definitely the work of a beginner. The Berlin genre picture dates from about 1510, the *Beheading of the Baptist* from around 1512. Paintings executed in the succeeding years, e.g. *St. Jerome* in Berlin and the *Virgin enthroned with Angels* in the same gallery or the *Card Game* at Wilton House, are done 250 with greater ease, are blond in colour and flowing, rather glazed in the painting.

We are very well acquainted with the art of Cornelis Engelbrechtsen, 245 who is regarded as Lucas's teacher, but we hesitate to designate specifically what the pupil owed to the teacher. For it is not impossible that in their relationship Lucas gave as well as received. Cornelis died in 1533, the same year as his illustrious pupil.

In the period between 1517 and 1531 Lucas produced pictures that vary considerably among themselves, and certainly show no trace of organic evolution. A small *Portrait of a Man* in a Dutch private collection[1]

*[1] Now in the Schloss Rohoncz Collection (Baron Thyssen), Lugano-Castagnola. The date is now read by Friedländer and other critics as 1511.

(The Hague, formerly in the Zeiss Collection, Berlin) dated 1517 gives a definite effect of chiaroscuro. The considerably more important *Portrait of a Man* in the Fry Collection, Bristol,[1] may date from about 1520. The imposing altarpiece with the *Last Judgement* in Leyden seems to date from about 1526, the sole work by the painter that has remained in his native town.[2] The condition of the triptych is by no means as bad as is usually stated. The rather ostentatious Renaissance design centres round the representation of nude bodies in movement. This is the period above all others when Lucas oscillates between two extremes. Local colours are often suppressed in favour of a dominant dull, earthy tone. Sometimes it even seems as if the draughtsman were neglecting the specific task of the painter as for instance in the carefully executed detail in the diptych of 1522 with the *Virgin, a Donor,* and the *Annunciation* (Munich, Pinakothek). At other times the interest is concentrated on a broad painterly treatment with strong patchy effects of light.

Lucas often found occasion to adopt in his paintings the rather chatty compositional style that he used with so much complacency in his engravings, as e.g. in the *Sermon* (Rijksmuseum, Amsterdam), in the *Moses striking Water from a Rock* at Nürnberg[3] or in the triptych in the Hermitage St. Petersburg, allegedly from the year 1531. The picture with the elaborate but rather confused composition showing Moses striking water out of the rock, dated 1527, painted on canvas and, like the majority of canvas pictures of the period, now dull and dark. came to the Nürnberg museum from Rome. Landscape and figures are firmly linked. The hero does not stand out clearly from the surroundings. The action is obscure. The last known painting by the master is in some respects also his most significant work. Though generally speaking the brush was less adaptable to his aims and moods than the burin—at the end of his meteor-like career, when there was scarcely anything left for Lucas the engraver to try, he marshalled all his forces once more in a painting. The subject of the *Healing of the Blind Man* is spread broadly over the central panel and the two wings of the triptych in St. Petersburg. Christ performs the miraculous cure in a wooded countryside, surrounded by a dense excited throng. The movements of the figures and even more the strong spotlight effect of the illumination bring life to the scene. This truly Dutch interest

Margin references:
254–260
261
252
249
VIII

*[1] Now in the National Gallery, London.

*[2] August 6, 1526, has been established as the actual date of the commission. The triptych was intended as a memorial for the Leyden alderman and councillor Claes Dircksz van Swieten (not as an altarpiece) and was already at its place near the font in St. Peter's Church, Leyden, before the end of 1527.

*[3] Now in the Museum of Fine Arts, Boston, Mass.

which is even more definite in the approximately contemporary paintings by Jan van Scorel, can be regarded as foreshadowing Rembrandt. A comparison between this *Healing of the Blind Man* and Rembrandt's *Hundred Guilder print* is not without interest.

Whether Lucas, who had certainly no further expectations to take with him to the grave as an engraver, would have progressed any further as a painter had not death put an end to his work is something that we may reasonably doubt. His ambition and his keen eye were certainly turned boldly into the distance but his foundation was not firm enough to assure a steadily increasing success. The people of Holland had first to liberate themselves and to define their political boundaries before their sense of realism could acquire the necessary restraint to develop a natural stylistic assurance. Without forcing the facts we can interpret the genius of Rembrandt as the fulfilment of many an aim that flickers dimly in the endeavour of his Leyden ancestor.

# JAN VAN SCOREL

THE opinions of the sixteenth century are unanimous on Jan van Scorel and proclaim his fame loudly and—the reasons for this fame. On the other hand, the judgment in more recent literature is full of doubt and criticism, because the value of his achievements, admired by his contemporaries, has now become questionable. So unbounded is our admiration for Netherlandish painting that Scorel's determined and conscious turning away from tradition seems at first sight to be a dangerous uprooting. In quite recent times, it is true, there is a dawning tendency to recognize the positive side of the Rome pilgrim's achievement—as we can see in Grete Ring's article.[1] The growing scientific spirit widens our susceptibilities in all directions. Increasing insight throws ever greater light on the necessity of change, and every result demands recognition. It may well be that behind this objectivity lurks the subjectivity of modern taste for which Scorel's mannerism has lost its horror. When the Obervellach altarpiece first became known, some forty years ago, this work, painted before the *Fall of Man*, was immediately placed far higher than all Scorel's later achievements. And since few people were able to examine this out-of-the-way triptych the bias in its favour was retained in the compilatory literature. The motive for Grete Ring's criticism of the early work was the desire to get rid of the foolish idea that on Italian soil the master had exchanged inherited values of priceless worth for a phantom. In reality, the style of the Obervellach altarpiece is discordant and on the verge of disintegration. One can sense the inner void and the readiness to receive fresh ideals.

Jan van Scorel was born on August 1, 1495, in the village of Schoorel near Alkmaar. His first teacher was Willem Cornelisz (more correctly Cornelis Willemsz), an unknown Haarlem painter,[2] and later he went to Amsterdam to Jacob Cornelisz. Restlessness and dissatisfaction with mere craftsmanship drove him to Jan Gossaert, who at that time—c. 1515—was at Utrecht and was looked upon, thanks to his Italian experience, as the great innovator. Subsequently, Scorel was lured southwards by his

242-244

---

[1] *Kunstchronik*, 17 May, 1918.

*[2] It is due to Professor J. Bruyn that we now have some idea of the art of Cornelis Willemsz (see D. P. R. A. Bouvy, in *Schilderkunst, Kerkelijke Kunst*, I, Bussum, 1965, p. 52, fig. V, A and B, and J. G. van Gelder, in *Simiolus*, I, 1967, p. 6, n. 10). Before he went to Cornelis Willemsz he may have been apprenticed to Cornelis Buys at Alkmaar, cf. Friedländer, *Die Altniederländische Malerei*, XII, 1935, p. 119.

love of travelling and his thirst for new experience and knowledge, to
Speyer 'where a cleric was skilled in architecture and perspective', to
Strasbourg, Basle and Nürnberg, where he may well have found understanding for his rationalistic ambitions in Dürer, then to Carinthia, where
in 1520—according to the inscription—he completed the Obervellach 264
altarpiece.

In that same year, the year of Raphael's death, he probably crossed
into Italy and stayed for some time at Venice. From there he made a
journey to the Holy Land, not merely as a pious pilgrim but also as a
mentally alert traveller eager to see the places where Christ's feet had
trodden. This painter's desire to interpret the biblical scene more
'correctly' than had been possible for his predecessors by expressing
time and place of the action in the costume, landscape and architecture
could not, of course, lead to results that would satisfy our modern
historical sense. Nevertheless, the endeavour played its part in forming
his style, in drawing him away from commonplace reality and in any
case, aided by memories of his travels, he was able to offer his contemporaries plausible novelty. The town of Jerusalem, painted in the landscape backgrounds of his religious pictures after studies from nature, was
viewed with awe and curiosity.                                    266

In Scorel's imagination, it is true, the Southern sun was blended with
Northern mists, the East with the West, biblical history with Roman
antiquity, the sacred figures of the gospels with the universally valid beauty
of antique statues, oriental materials cut to antique patterns.

Scorel returned to Venice from the East, visited several other Italian
towns and finally reached Rome where, under the brief rule of Hadrian
VI, from January 9, 1522 to September 14, 1523—a breathing space in
the Roman High Renaissance—he enjoyed a favoured position as a com-
patriot of the Utrecht-born pope, and was placed 'over het heel Belvider'.
Scorel was still in Rome on May 26, 1524, as is evident from a letter
with that date. However he returned to his Northern home shortly after
and settled at Utrecht where, held in high esteem, he remained until his
death on December 6, 1562, with only brief interruptions to work at
Haarlem and Delft. Short as his stay in Rome was, it made a decisive and
lasting impression on his entire production. As a result of his Dutch temperament when he tried to become a Roman he became a Venetian.

Since the master's chief religious works, which once stood at Utrecht,
Haarlem, Gouda and Delft, have all perished, we are forced to establish our
views of his art on panels laboriously collected in critical research. A large
altarpiece stands, unnoticed, in the main church at Breda.          267–268

The determination to make radical changes, the ambitious thirst for originality, the pleasure in surprising inventions form the mainspring of his endeavour; the course was set by his interest in antiquarian accuracy and his enthusiasm for antique sculpture. The human body is freed from the fetters of many-layered costumes, is shown in the nude or in flowing drapery which, moulded on the human form, seems to expose rather than veil the organism beneath. With statuary as his model the painter strives to find uniform and impressive movements, in easy contraposto, that can dominate the position, steps and gestures of each figure.

The religious pictures are endowed with dignity and monumentality by a regular formation of the healthy muscular forms, a stately carriage, pathos of attitude and a 'beauty' in the heads that is derived from the art of others. The reverent attitude of mind, that pieced everything together, bit by bit, with loving care and, despite the overall unnaturalness, forced illusion on the details, is completely abandoned in favour of the picture conceived as a whole and the correctness of the proportions. Scorel treats the details perfunctorily. He expresses himself rather in the movements of the body than in the features of the face. His heads, little individualized, often appear mask-like.

Jan Gossaert, who had looked around in Rome some fifteen years before Scorel and had then returned to the Netherlands as teacher and guide to the new aims, was primarily gifted as a draughtsman, goldsmith and sculptor. Scorel viewed space peopled with statues with the eye of a painter. In his scrupulous regard for all formal factors Gossaert remained tied to the Netherlandish tradition, Scorel in step with the Italian High Renaissance style, concentrated on the picture as a whole. Gossaert is painfully exact, analytical and pedantic, Scorel hasty, fluent and dynamic. For Gossaert light is a means to an end, the end being the illusion of three-dimensional form, whereas Scorel builds up his picture in light and shade, which are the essential elements; his shadows are deep, cover wide areas, often ruthlessly dominating the form. Classic profiles not infrequently stand out effectively as flat discs against the light background. Gossaert came from Maubeuge, was Latin or at least half-Latin, whereas Scorel was Dutch with a sensitive eye for light and tone values. His acute inventiveness proceeds from light contrasts, he accentuates and suppresses and composes with light. The golden shimmer of his misty backgrounds anticipates the intentions of Aelbert Cuyp; the all-enshrouding darkness of his interiors can be regarded as the germ of Rembrandtesque chiaroscuro. Scorel, who observed what was far off rather than what was close, whose ideals were colourless stone figures and reliefs, was indifferent and arbitrary in his treatment of local colour. His palette, which contains broken colours, is harmonious and blond though sometimes rent by an excessive contrast of light and shade.

Scorel developed his manner of painting to suit the purpose of his design, independently and consistently. The colour is soft, broadly applied in large patches, his pigment is transparent and enamel-like but not excessively smooth. He expresses the swift-gliding mobility of shadows with a stippling brush, illumines and spotlights the forms. In places the light chews up the line and softens it.

Despite all novelty, grandeur and ideality this master's devotional pictures remain bare, like an egg that has been drained dry; the content, namely the religious feeling, has escaped. Presumably the Jerusalem pilgrim, favourite of the pope, Utrecht canon was an orthodox believer whose art was reverently dedicated to God. But general outlook and creed do not suffice; the profanation, externalization and inner emptiness of the religious picture was a necessary result of his way of seeing and his manner of composing. Scorel transformed the devotional picture into a history piece in the grand 'manner'.

Recently two works by Scorel have come to light, accredited from a reference by van Mander. First the *Presentation in the Temple*, acquired by 265 Gustav Glück for the Vienna gallery, and secondly a fragment discovered by Grete Ring at Valenciennes. The *Presentation* is evidently identical with the picture once owned by Geert Schoterbosch at Haarlem which was admired by van Mander for its magnificent architecture. The fragment with the *Martyrdom of St. Lawrence* certainly formed part of the altarpiece of this saint at Marchiennes in the Artois, mentioned in the same source.[1]

The two panels provide a welcome addition to our knowledge. Though, admittedly, there is no lack of altar panels to show the master's compositional style, types and general conception, in view of the tremendous prestige that he enjoyed as an artist and in view of the heavy demands on

*[1] The fragment with the *Martyrdom of St. Lawrence*, which until the First World War was in the Museum of Valenciennes, has since disappeared. In his most important article on late works by Scorel in France and Flanders (referred to on p. 128, note 2) Professor van Gelder has published an old copy of the complete composition which he identified in the Museum of Poznan. The *Martyrdom of St. Lawrence* was one of three altarpieces by Scorel which, according to van Mander, were in the Abbey Church of Marchiennes. Among these three altarpieces, which were commissioned by Jacques Coëne, abbot of Marchiennes 1501–1542, the largest, with two pairs of movable wings, was dedicated to St. Stephen and St. James. It was painted about 1541. Except for one static wing and the central panel with the *Stoning of St. Stephen*, this altarpiece has been reconstituted at the Museum of Douai by its curator, M. J. Guillouet, who published it in *Oud-Holland*, LXXIX/2, 1964, pp. 89–98. A drawing of the *Stoning of St. Stephen* in the F. Lugt Collection, Paris, is, according to van Gelder, the design for the lost painting. The third altarpiece by Scorel at Marchiennes mentioned by van Mander was a triptych with *St. Ursula and the 11,000 Virgins*, the right wing of which has recently been found by M. Guillouet (see van Gelder, in *Simiolus*, op. cit., p. 22).

his workshop we must from the outset reckon with copies, imitations and the collaboration of pupils. Only the best works can give an idea of Scorel's manner of painting and personal handwriting. These do not include, for example the *Crucifixion* in the Bonn museum, which owing to its problematic inscription 'Schoorle 1530' is often quoted in the literature, **275** but they do include the *Magdalen* in Amsterdam. The positive and special qualities of his style are better illustrated in the *Magdalen* than in any other of his compositions. The general effect of sunniness and humidity in the picture is striking, and dominates both the plastic volume and the local colours. The Magdalen was frequently portrayed by his contemporaries and fellow-countrymen but generally within a narrow framework, scarcely ever, as here, in a wide landscape setting. The gradation of the tone values, the aerial perspective, the lights flashing in dots and strips, the cast shadows are all observed for their own sake and rendered with brilliance and transparent luminosity. The deep cast shadows in the drapery sometimes swamp the individual folds. Bright patches gleam out, e.g. in the tree trunk on the right but without defining the cylindrical form of the trunk. The areas of shadow are not sharply edged but soft against the sky. The texture of hair and drapery is characterized with sensitive perception. The extensive use of glazes is adapted to characterize the material, thin in places, particularly in the flesh where the drawing shines through, and in places oily and with impasto. Light, air and landscape are used as the chief expressive factors and confer ideality and festive distinction on the attractive woman.

All Scorel's characteristics become virtues in his portraits. The nature of the task brings him back to the particular. The emancipation from tradition, which was a danger for his religious painting, is an advantage here because the subdued, limited and monotonous gravity, a rudiment of the donor portrait, is lifted and a study of human nature introduced. Scorel's portraits differ from one another in carriage, posture and movement of the hands. The self-confident free personality of the sixteenth century is portrayed with deep insight into the human mind. Scorel had seen the world, was versed in languages, and, moreover, a musician and a poet. He does not seek out physical facts with minute detail and completeness but rather surveys the whole and grasps the essential features by selecting a certain turn of the head, carriage of the body, movement of the hand to suit the temperament of the sitter and a lighting that gives surprising emphasis to the structure of the head. He expresses the inner life of the individual with keen insight. Scorel's beings are communicative, open their hearts to us with eloquence.

The richness and variety of his portraiture is revealed in the long series of *Jerusalem Pilgrims* in the Utrecht Museum, although the panels have suffered considerably and are disfigured by extensive retouching. This great achievement of Dutch portraiture, which we are able to date— two groups shortly after 1525, one soon after 1535 and one after 1541— this vigorous root of the guild group-portrait, that flourished so luxuriantly in the seventeenth century, represents the starting-point and standard of judgment. A thorough study of the surviving parts is highly instructive.

The portrait frieze in the Haarlem museum, which shows twelve Jerusalem pilgrims, is better preserved than the Utrecht groups. Fairly  269 early, to judge by the style not later than the twenties, and obviously by the same hand as the Utrecht groups, that is by Scorel, this work gives so much variety to the turn of the heads, the direction of the eyes and the individual expressions that it should form the basis for our assessment of the master's portrait painting. Here if anywhere the keen unbiassed power of observation of the Netherlander combines with the dignity and freedom of the Italian High Renaissance. Though they are closer together the men are encompassed by air and each figure stands out fully modelled, thanks mainly to the consistent treatment of the lighting. The members of the company are depicted with a confident glance, a strongly expressive mouth-line, with a natural reverence, varied according to the character and temperament of the individual.

The heads are given in half-profile and for the most part are so strongly illumined that the far side of the face is profiled as a light patch against the dark background, but powerfully articulated by broad shadows along the bridge of the nose and on the cheeks. In some parts the shadows are sharply delineated, in others they terminate in softly blurred edges, everywhere lightly poised on the forms.

Generally speaking the pathos in the individual portraits, mainly achieved by the lighting, is less marked than in the group portraits, where the chiaroscuro, whilst holding the members together, also gives emphasis and variety to the monotonous chain of figures.

Of the well-known and often quoted single portraits the one of Agatha van Schoonhoven in Rome, in particular, is an instructive example (by  274 way of exception signed, and dated 1529). The young roguish, lovingly devoted woman is portrayed with an astonishing concentration on the essentials, with a directness that recalls Frans Hals.

Outstanding among several portraits that have only recently come to light is the *Portrait of a Jerusalem Pilgrim* which passed from a private

273 collection in Trier to the Nürnberg collector R. Chillingworth.[1] To judge
by the costume and the hat with the broad brim, the portrait must date
from shortly after 1520. Eyes and eloquent gesture point with restrained
yearning into the distance so that the background landscape with its
outlandish buildings seems more than a superficial addition. The *Portrait*
272 *of a Man* in the Berlin museum achieves even greater harmony and
delicacy of expression, in this instance one of solicitous devotion; on the
reverse is a statuesque figure of *Lucretia*. We have here one half of a
diptych the other half of which was a panel with the Virgin. Lucretia,
to be sure, is a strange adjunct to a Madonna.

Other portraits just as certainly by Scorel are at Turin, in the collec-
281, 282 tion of the Earl of Pembroke,[2] privately owned at Wiesbaden,[2] on the
Berlin art market; further there is a *Portrait of a Child* at Bergamo and one
271 at Rotterdam, the former a mischievous boy, the latter a well-behaved
model schoolboy, and the *Man with the Dog*,[2] where empty arrogance is
drastically expressed, in Cologne.

Scorel's art made a powerful impression throughout Holland and can
be traced in three strong currents in Amsterdam. In the portraits of Dirk
Jacobsz, who was a son of his old teacher Jacob Cornelisz, we find a
willing acceptance of the Utrecht master's influence. Marten van
277–278 Heemskerck's excited extravagances have their origin in Scorel as has the
immaculate perfection to which the portrait painting of Anthony Mor
aspired. In their earlier works these two pupils are so close to their master
that the attribution of certain paintings oscillates from one to another.
276 The *Family Group* in Cassel, for all its daring an intimate depiction of
279–280 domestic happiness, and the *Portraits of Pieter Bicker and his Wife* belonging
to Baron Schimmelpenninck[3] (dated 1529?), seem to transcend Scorel's
limits in their exuberant vitality. But we must credit the master with
great versatility as a portraitist. And taking everything into consideration
I should prefer to regard him as the author rather than Heemskerck with
his arbitrary bravura and superficial greatness, just as I am inclined to
credit him, rather than Anthony Mor, with the group portrait of the
five *Jerusalem Pilgrims* in Utrecht.

[*1] Now in the Museum of the Cranbrook Academy of Arts, Bloomfield Hills, Michigan.
[*2] These portraits are now attributed by Friedländer and other scholars to Jan Cornelisz
Vermeyen, an artist whose *œuvre* has been assembled only quite recently. That from Wiesbaden,
a portrait of Erard de la Marck, Bishop of Liège, is now in the Rijksmuseum, Amsterdam.
[*3] They are now in the Rijksmuseum, Amsterdam. The completely different character of a
portrait by Scorel, also dated 1529, which came to light only after 1935, led Friedländer later to
express even greater doubts as to Scorel's authorship, and to consider the attribution to Heemskerck rather favourably. See Friedländer, *Die Altniederländische Malerei*, XIV, 1937, p. 129.

# PIETER BRUEGEL

IN every one of Jan van Eyck's works, more, in every part of any work, in every head, every hand, his greatness can be demonstrated. His masterly observation and interpretation is concentrated in each detail and it is in this mastery that his historical importance lies.

In our eagerness to reveal Pieter Bruegel's greatness we should like to line up everything by the master we can lay our hands on—with the uneasy feeling that with every work of his that has perished something of his title to fame has perished too. But our desire to proclaim his worth is all the more intense because not many art lovers have a full idea of the extent and richness of his creative power. The master does not seem to occupy his rightful place in the public mind. It is to be feared that even to mention Jan van Eyck and Bruegel in one breath may sound provocative.

There is more than one painter named Bruegel, Brueghel or Breughel. But the family produced only one great master. And he was the eldest, the founder of the dynasty, Pieter, nicknamed 'Peasant-Bruegel'.

The second Pieter Brueghel was nothing but an imitator and copyist who lived on his father's heritage, whilst Jan, the other son, though more independent, was yet a painter of lesser stature. The elder master spelt his name (with but few exceptions): Bruegel, the sons preferred the spelling Brueghel.

Bruegel is the name of a place. There are two villages of that name, either possible as the birth-place of the painter; both lie east of Antwerp, the one not far from Hertogenbosch, the other further south in the province of Limburg.

The name 'Peeter Brueghels' appears in the Antwerp guild list of 1551. At that time the painter became free master. He died in Brussels in 1569. With the aid of van Mander's account, and a variety of combinations, attempts have been made to complete his biography. Bruegel is alleged to have been a pupil of Pieter Coeck van Alost in Antwerp and to have married his teacher's daughter Maria, whom he had carried in his arms when she was a child. So van Mander relates. Maria, Coeck's daughter, cannot have been born before 1540 or (since she married in 1563) after 1545. If we accept the story that Bruegel carried the child in his arms when he was an apprentice, then the years of his apprenticeship must have been roughly between 1540 and 1545. If he entered Coeck's work-shop at the customary age, then the year of his birth must lie somewhere between 1528 and 1530.

Bruegel's portrait has survived in engravings and they show him with a dignified and patrician air. If he were born in 1530 he would have been only thirty-nine when he died in 1569. He looks a little older. We will therefore have to push the year of his birth back as far as possible, even further than 1525. Moreover, all conclusions based on his apprenticeship with Coeck are doubtful because van Mander's information cannot be confirmed in any way. Bruegel is not entered as a pupil in the Antwerp guild lists. Perhaps the lists have not come down to us complete. Stylistic criticism brings no manner of confirmation. From the erudite art of Coeck we can span no bridge to Bruegel.[1] From a study of Bruegel's beginnings, or what seem to us beginnings, we might even be tempted to believe that he was never trained by a professional panel painter, least of all by Coeck. Perhaps van Mander only heard that Bruegel had married Coeck's daughter and added the rest himself. But if Bruegel did not serve his apprenticeship with Coeck, and not even in Antwerp, then many possibilities open up and the artist who appears in Antwerp in 1551 could have previously worked as master elsewhere.

Bruegel's relationship to Jerome Bosch is as close as his link with Pieter Coeck is slight. The master of Hertogenbosch, though not Bruegel's master, is certainly his ancestor, in fact his only ancestor with whom he has any affinity—at any rate as far as we can tell from our knowledge of the older art. Bosch died in 1516. At that time Bruegel, even if he was already alive, would scarcely have been old enough to be anyone's pupil. But in view of the fact that the village where he may have been born is not far from Hertogenbosch we can quite well imagine that his first impressions were formed on Bosch's art, that he was apprenticed to a follower of Bosch, and that the affinity is based on a community of race and stock. On the other hand the relationship between the two masters could be explained in a different and more superficial way. During his first years in Antwerp Bruegel worked for the print publisher Jerome Cock. This publisher had had compositions by Bosch reproduced as prints. As a shrewd businessman he may have recognized Bruegel's talent as a designer of didactic and entertaining popular prints and have

*1 Connections between the art of Bruegel and Coeck have been shown to exist by several scholars and last by F. Grossmann, in *Festschrift Kurt Badt zum siebzigsten Geburtstag*, Berlin, 1961, pp. 135 ff., where earlier literature on the subject is also listed, and by G. Marlier, *La Renaissance flamande, Pierre Coeck d'Alost*, Brussels, 1966, *passim*.

IX. Pieter Bruegel: *Children's Games*. Detail. Vienna, Kunsthistorisches Museum

referred him to the example of the great artist then dead, whose compositions he had disseminated so profitably.

Jerome Cock could also have been directly responsible for the direction
his print designer's art took. There has recently come to the Berlin print
room a drawing by Cock with the remarkably early date 1541, a *Landscape with St. Jerome*, which, like his etchings, is similar in conception
to Bruegel's landscapes. The drawing, however, is not signed 'Jerome'
but only 'Cock' and could thus be the work of Matthys Cock his brother,
of whom van Mander speaks in very emphatic terms.

The period during which Bruegel became master in Antwerp was a
critical one in the history of Netherlandish art. Painters such as Floris
and Coxie were beginning to dominate the scene. Everything that seems
genuine and fruitful to us today was then merely an undercurrent.
Bruegel does not appear to have been regarded as a great artist by his
contemporaries. His art lacked the grand style, lacked Roman erudition,
in a word everything that made the craftsman painter an artist—the
conception 'artist' only came up at that time. For the older generation
Bruegel's art lacked the careful finish and enamel-like technique, whilst
the younger generation may have frowningly wondered why Bruegel's
visit to Italy had so entirely failed to improve his taste.

Bruegel did visit Italy. Not only does van Mander say: "he travelled
to France and thence to Italy". On certain engravings and drawings
dated 1553 the name of the place is given as *Romae*.

During his lifetime Bruegel's art appealed mainly to the man in the
street and more through the content than through the form. He instructed
the people, delighted and entertained them, a public that enjoyed robust
humour and caricature. With rather unskilled prints after his drawings he
satisfied an uninformed longing for pictures and he drew inspiration from
the eternal sources of popular imagination whilst on a higher level, and
on the surface, Netherlandish painting was being paralysed by Roman-
izing culture.

Bruegel, like so many painters of Germanic origin, was at bottom a
draughtsman and illustrator. He began as a designer for engravings and
trained himself to become an easy and witty story-teller before he began to
paint pictures. In a good as well as in a bad sense the training left its mark
on the design and technique of his paintings. In 1551 he became master,
but the first signed and dated picture known to us is from the year 1558.[1]

*[1] A *Landscape with the Parable of the Sower*, now in the Timken Art Gallery, San Diego, California,
and first mentioned by Friedländer (in *Pantheon*, 1931, p. 58), bears the date 1557 and recently a
*Landscape with Christ appearing to the Apostles at the Sea of Tiberias*, signed and dated 1553, and

It is possible to separate the period of the drawings: before 1558, from the period of the paintings: 1558 to 1569, the year of his death.

There is one—not quite certain—exception, a picture signed 'Bruegel' and dated 1556. This is the *Operation for the Stone* which was sold with the von Gerhard Collection, Berlin, in 1911.[1] The panel is 29 by 40 inches. Inside a village barber's shop the operation is being performed in varying ways on the heads of the patients. What is related here at length, in a rather wild and clumsy genre manner, was given a symbolic twist by Bosch in his more pointed way (cf. his picture in the Prado). In spite of the evident weaknesses, the signature—P. Bruegel 1556—which is exact in style and spelling, seems to confirm the authenticity of the picture. The large number of surviving copies of the master's pictures do not generally agree with the originals in the style of the signature and in the date. This isolated painting is too slight and too uncertain as a basis for our ideas of Bruegel's painting around 1556.

Bruegel begins as an imitator of Bosch, begins as a draughtsman and —presumably stimulated by the brothers Matthys and Jerome Cock— as a landscape artist. On his journey—c. 1553—he, as a Netherlander, is absorbed by the novelty of Alpine scenery. In Italy he is impressed by landscape and topography but not, as far as we can see, by the art of the Italian High Renaissance.

From 1558 on Bruegel considers himself a painter and overcomes progressively the habits of the illustrator. Paintings, like picture-sheets, overcrowded in content and form, such as the *Proverbs* in Berlin, and the IX *Children's Games* in Vienna, are dated 1559 and 1560; the simple genre pieces, with few large figures and readily intelligible themes, with a uniform spatial composition and pictorially conceived design, such as the 287, 290 *Peasant Wedding* and the *Peasant Dance* in Vienna seem to round off his lifework and to be the goal of his aims. Bruegel's art becomes increasingly free of the influence of Bosch. The contrast, which is a contrast of generations, becomes more pronounced the more Bruegel succeeds in establishing his own easy-going, even humorous interpretation of reality in opposition to the allegorizing and moralizing tendency dictated by the taste of the time and by the publisher.

Much of Bruegel's work has undoubtedly perished, particularly his water colour paintings on fine canvas. Still more would have been destroyed had not Habsburg princes shown an early taste for the peasant

accepted by Friedländer as an original work of the master, has been published by Ch. de Tolnay in *The Burlington Magazine*, XCVII, 1955, pp. 239 ff.

*[1] Later in the Tomcsányi Collection, Budapest. See also p. 139 note 5.

painter. Just as Philip II loved Bosch's inventions with their significance and mystery, so Rudolph II and Archduke Leopold Wilhelm delighted in Bruegel's work. It is to this interest, remarkable as a historical and psychological phenomenon, that we owe the preservation of a substantial part of Bruegel's *oeuvre*. Netherlandish robustness, directness and honesty acted as a counterfoil to the religious discipline and to the rigours of Spanish court etiquette. Bruegel's pictures may have, to some extent, replaced the court jester.

Almost half the surviving works by the master—if we take the quality into consideration more than half—are in the Vienna museum. In Vienna, there are fifteen pictures by his hand in the gallery, and one privately owned,[1] four in Brussels,[2] one in Berlin,[3] one in the Louvre, none in England, as far as I can see (I do not believe that the Northwick Park picture is genuine),[4] one privately owned in Hungary,[5] one in Copenhagen,[6] two in Munich, two in Naples, two privately owned in Antwerp, one in the Prado, one in the Darmstadt museum, one in the Lobkowitz collection at Raudnitz,[7] one in Montpellier[8]—that makes in all thirty-four originals.[9] I regard all the rest as doubtful.

283–293

The Vienna collections give a full picture of Bruegel's art. There we find landscapes, biblical subjects and genre-like pieces. The categories cannot be clearly segregated. A biblical content is infused into the landscape and all human activities are conceived as genre. Innumerable figures, a whole world, adventure, picturesque scenes, gaiety and edification, an endless spectacle unfolds, entertaining for the simple observer, a miracle for one who is following the course of Netherlandish art.

Convention and tradition are overcome. Nothing remains of the mood of the early Netherlandish devotional panel which was fashioned bit by

*[1] This picture, *The Adoration of the Kings*, is now in the National Gallery, London.
*[2] In addition to the four paintings in the Royal Museum, there is now one in a private collection in Brussels.
*[3] The Berlin museum now owns two paintings by Bruegel.
*[4] The Northwick Park picture, which Friedländer admitted to the list of autograph works in *Die Altniederländische Malerei*, XIV, 1937, p. 60, is now in the Musée Municipal, Brussels. From the 1937 list three are now in England; to these must be added two undoubted originals, now in the collection of Count Antoine Seilern, London, which have come to light since 1937.
*[5] There is now one painting by Bruegel in the Museum of Fine Arts, Budapest. The *Operation for the Stone*, the authenticity of which appeared highly doubtful to Friedländer in 1937, was last heard of in the Tomcsányi Collection, Budapest.
*[6] Two according to Friedländer's list of 1937.
*[7] This picture is now in the National Gallery, Prague.
*[8] No longer regarded as a work of Bruegel by Friedländer or any other authority.
*[9] Friedländer's list of 1937 contains fifty paintings. It is made up of the works referred to in the text and in the preceding notes and of ten more, which are now in Rome (one), Holland (three), Switzerland (two), and U.S.A. (four); it should, however, be added, that several of the works accepted by Friedländer as autograph have been doubted by other scholars.

bit from the model; nothing is left of the lingering observation in which figures and groups were isolated and observed details of nature pieced together in wondrous manner. Nor do Italian compositional laws prevail. Bruegel is free of Romanist ambitions, more so than any other painter of his day, he seems to be consciously opposed to the aims of his contemporaries and compatriots.

There was in Bruegel, in addition to his delight in direct observation of nature, in addition to his bent for story-telling, also defiant craving for novelty. Suspicious of every formula, of all ceremonial, estranged from the old gods, inimical to the new ones, the master liked nothing better than to peer ever closer into what was sacred, until the human and commonplace core was exposed, or to move ever farther away from greatness until it became insignificant and void. He was for ever seeking a new angle, a new side, a wider vantage point.

The master's eloquence was continually in flux. He never repeated himself. Compelled by the overflowing richness of his own ideas he had no time to work out the details. Everything drove him to haste, the manner of his illustration, the fire of his personality, the perpetual urge to show something new. He became an impressionist as a result of his own temperament and produced a style that satisfied the rhythm of his own nature.

His ability to grasp movement is obvious, his inventive imagination is so rich that amongst a thousand figures no two appear in the same attitude. Compared with Bruegel's people, the creatures produced by those artists who have on occasion been mentioned as his predecessors— such as Lucas van Leyden, Pieter Aertsen, Hemessen and even Bosch— seem, for all their would-be animation, feeble, monotonous, rigid, posing.

If we do compare Bruegel's eye with the photographic lens then we must not forget to add that Bruegel always seized the critical moment in the movement whereas it is just this moment that the camera rarely captures and then only by chance. No observation, however keen, however patient, could give this ability; it was the result of a brilliantly intuitive understanding of the functioning of the human body.

When representing the human form, older artists started with the straight and upright figure, with a fundamental idea based more on knowledge than on observation. Attempts were made, more or less successfully with the aid of particular studies from nature, to enrich the norm by a displacement, a foreshortening, an inclination, a turn. Bruegel, on the other hand, never seems to apply foreshortening to an ideal figure, but begins with the action, and from one particular angle seizes the ever-changing contour as a whole. Therein lies the secret of the manifold variety of movement, of his ability to make the activity and motive power of his people convincing.

Working in the spirit of the Italian Renaissance, the Netherlandish artists of the sixteenth century started out with the nude figure. Clothing was arranged on the framework of the body, revealing or concealing, and subordinated to it. For Bruegel no such dualism exists. Body and dress casually associated, are seen as an entity.

Bruegel's figures generally appear squat, seen from above in foreshortening, broad and clumsy yet agile, coiled together, in endless diversity of outlines not one of which in any way recalls the academical basis: the erect nude figure, the proud beauty of the upright body.

He is a pioneer in the boldness with which he overlooks the details, in the way he visualizes the relationship of the parts to one another. He abandons the traditional Netherlandish detailed and exhaustive drawing, modelling and characterization of texture. His origins as a draughtsman, his black and white graphic phase, may have fostered this indifference to detail. The vital thing is his eye for the whole. The forms are firmly contoured. The master is not even afraid to give a linear emphasis to the outlines so as to enhance the expression. This solidity in the drawing combined with a primitive and positive use of local colours lends his pictures a superficial archaism and a popular robustness. By weakening the modelling he intensifies the effect of the silhouette. Bruegel does not introduce original motifs into traditional compositional schemata but aims rather at an overall originality in the design of the pictorial theme.

In the art of the fifteenth century if the human beings are large the landscape is small. The human being is in the centre of interest, in the foreground. Everything else is purely accessory, a mere filling for the space and the ground. Landscape remains of lesser importance even when at the beginning of the sixteenth century, it commences to form the content of a new art category. Bruegel reverses the relationship, and here too he proceeds to the limit. Like a pantheist who delights in ever new visions, he seems to mock at the anthropocentric outlook. He gives to the landscape what he takes away from man. Whilst reducing the human being to ant-like unimportance he swells the landscape to gigantic stature. There is width and depth in his landscapes which, despite some fantastic details, are organically constructed after nature, or rather in the spirit of nature. When he crossed the Alps on his journey to Italy Bruegel may have been so deeply impressed with their grandeur that his eye rejected the normal standards. Carel van Mander does not express himself at all badly when he remarks "at that time the master swallowed the mountains and rocks of the Alps and later spat them out in his pictures."

Admittedly, the landscape painters of the sixteenth century who worked as specialists in this field—Bruegel was certainly no specialist—loved the picturesque richness of the high mountains but they fashioned greatness with poverty of spirit. Their piled-up masses and exaggerations lack the impetuosity of Bruegel's creations. Their steep and jagged rocks extend and rise monotonously parallel to the picture plane, whereas Bruegel drives his formations diagonally into the depths and opens up astonishing vistas.

In as far as Patenier and his followers were able at all to express mood in landscape they were absorbed in the idyllic spirit of mid-summer. Bruegel, on the other hand, perceives the spirit of every season and in his pictures expresses the turbulence of early spring as well as the steely clarity of winter. Landscape for him is more than just something to be looked at. Nature reveals herself to him in all her changing relationship to humanity, now harsh and inhospitable, now richly bountiful, but always dominant and all-embracing.

Genre motifs had begun to twine round the stem of religious art even in the Middle Ages. Painters in the fifteenth century were already solving specifically genre problems and at the beginning of the sixteenth century there were already specialists in the field of genre painting. But it was long before the true spirit of genre emerged freely. Peasant Bruegel was the first successfully to eliminate the lingering echo of religious devotion, the expression of solemn gravity in the heads and gestures. He was the first to observe the daily round of human activity with unprejudiced honesty, with humour but without mockery or distortion and without bias. Even in Bosch's art mankind, if not striving towards Heaven, is at least heading for Hell.

The reader who has followed these remarks may well ask what exactly was left for the painters of the seventeenth century to achieve since their predecessor had penetrated victoriously so far.

Bruegel, compared with, say, Brouwer, is more a draughtsman than a painter. In his ever-present endeavour to outline the action, to seize and define the passing movement, he lays no great weight on the subtleties of line or colour. He is more interested in the physical than in the psychological side, in the type rather than in the individual. The comical, sly peasant heads with large round eyes are not individualized as portraits. But as Bruegel avoids large-scale figures the generalized emptiness of the heads does not disturb us unduly. And the irresistible momentum of the whole leaves the onlooker no time to criticize the details. Bruegel's interest did not lie in a penetrating study of human individuality. He is almost the only great Netherlandish artist whose *oeuvre* does not include portraiture.

Despite all imperfections—the newly conquered territory was too vast for the conquerer to dominate it completely—Bruegel is one of the great ones in the historic sequence. And to place him alongside Jan van Eyck and Rembrandt is to emphasize what is essential in the course of Netherlandish painting.

PIETER BRUEGEL: The Painter and the Connoisseur. Drawing, about 1568.
*Vienna, Albertina*

# THE SIXTEENTH CENTURY

160. Bernaert van Orley: *The Ruin of the Children of Job*. Brussels, Museum

51. BERNAERT VAN ORLEY: *The Poor Lazarus at the Door of the Rich Man; The Death of the Rich Man and his Torments in Hell.* Wings of the Job altarpiece. Brussels, Museum

162. BERNAERT VAN ORLEY: *Charles V*. Budapest, Museum

163. Bernaert van Orley. *Dr. Georg van Zelle*. Brussels, Museum

164. QUENTIN MASSYS: *Virgin and Child*. Brussels, Museum

165. QUENTIN MASSYS: *The Rest on the Flight into Egypt*. Worcester, Mass., Art Museum

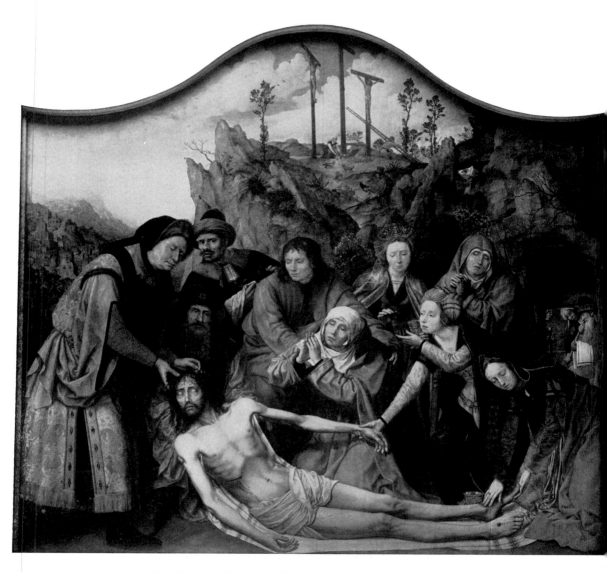

166. QUENTIN MASSYS: *The Entombment*. Antwerp, Museum

167. Quentin Massys: *The Holy Kindred*. Centre panel of the St. Anne altarpiece. Brussels, Museum

168. QUENTIN MASSYS: *The Death of the Virgin*.
Right wing of the St. Anne altarpiece. Brussels, Museum

169. Quentin Massys: *St. Mary Magdalen*. Antwerp, Museum

170. Quentin Massys: *Christ presented to the People*. Madrid, Prado

171. Quentin Massys: *The Holy Trinity and Virgin and Child*. Centre panel of an altarpiece.
Munich, Alte Pinakothek

173. QUENTIN MASSYS: *A Man*. Edinburgh,
National Gallery of Scotland

172. QUENTIN MASSYS: *A Man*. Frankfurt,
Staedel Institute

174–175. QUENTIN MASSYS: *A Man and his Wife.* Oldenburg, Museum

176. Quentin Massys: *A Man with a Pink*. Chicago, Art Institute

177. QUENTIN MASSYS: *A Money Changer and his Wife*. Paris, Louvre

178. QUENTIN MASSYS: *Erasmus of Rotterdam*. Rome, Galleria Corsini

179. Quentin Massys: *Petrus Aegidius*. Longford Castle, Earl of Radnor

180 QUENTIN MASSYS and PATENIER: *The Temptation of St. Anthony*. Madrid, Prado

181. Patenier: *The Rest on the Flight into Egypt*. Madrid, Prado

183. PATENIER: *Charon crossing the Styx. M*

184. PATENIER: *The Baptism of Christ*. Vienna, Kunsthistorisches Museum

185. PATENIER: *The Flight into Egypt.* Antwerp, Museum

186. HERRI MET DE BLES: *The Flight into Egypt.* London, Hallsborough Gallery

187. CORNELIS MASSYS: *St. Jerome in the Wilderness*. Antwerp, Museum

188. CORNELIS MASSYS: *The Virgin and St. Joseph arriving at the Inn in Bethlehem.*
Berlin-Dahlem, Staatliche Museen

189. MASTER OF THE FEMALE HALF-LENGTHS: *Three Ladies making Music*. Vienna, Harrach Collection

190. MASTER OF THE FEMALE HALF-LENGTHS: *The Adoration of the Kings*. Regensburg, Museum

191. YSENBRANDT: *The Seven Sorrows of the Virgins*. Bruges, Notre-Dame

193. Joos van Cleve: *Woman with a Rosary*. Florence, Uffizi

192. Ysenbrandt: *The Gold-Weigher*. New York, Metropolitan Museum of Art

195. Joos van Cleve: *Queen Eleanor of France*.
Vienna, Kunsthistorisches Museum

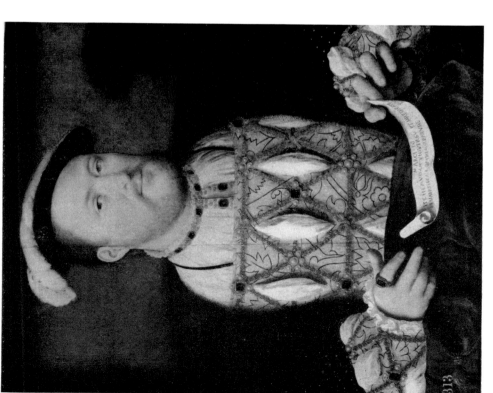

194. Joos van Cleve: *Henry VIII*. Hampton Court Palace.
Reproduced by gracious permission of Her Majesty The Queen

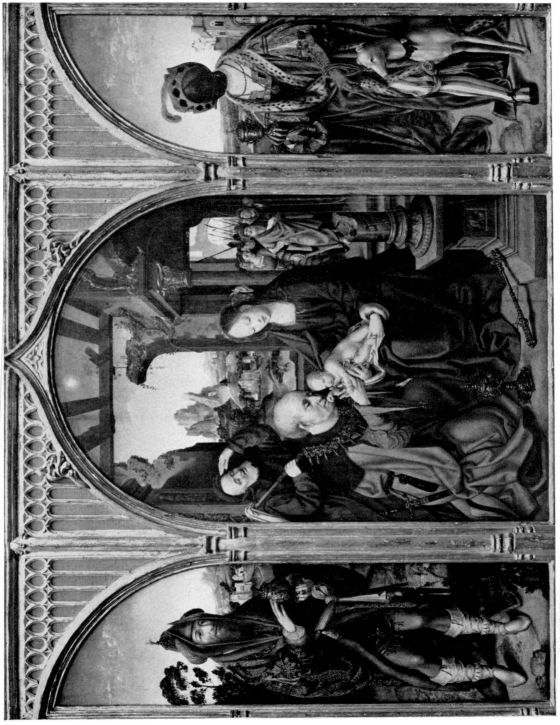

126. JOOS VAN CLEVE: *The Adoration of the Kings.* Detroit Institute of Arts

197. Joos van Cleve: *The Death of the Virgin.* Centre panel of a triptych. Munich, Alte Pinakothek

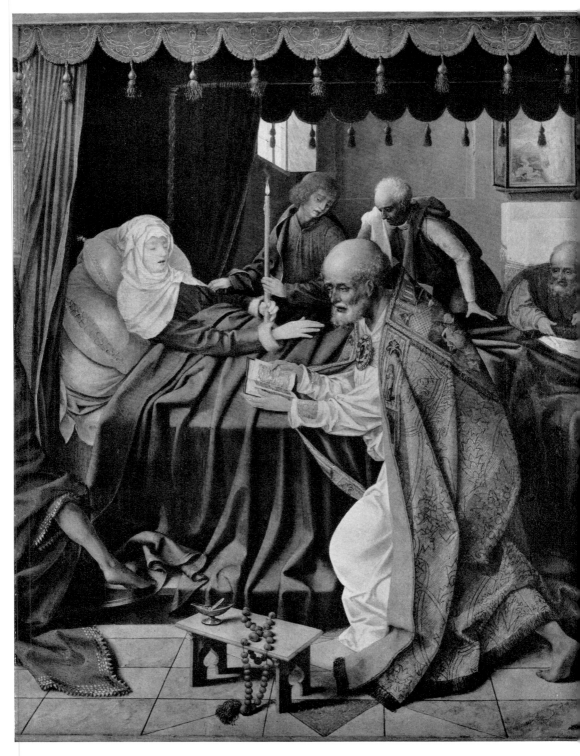

198. JOOS VAN CLEVE: *The Death of the Virgin* (detail). Centre panel of a triptych.
Cologne, Wallraf-Richartz Museum

199. Joos van Cleve: *The Holy Family*. Vienna, Kunsthistorisches Museum

200. JOOS VAN CLEVE: *Virgin and Child with Angels*. Lulworth Castle, Colonel J. Weld

201. JOOS VAN CLEVE: *The Rest on the Flight into Egypt*. Brussels, Museum

202. JOOS VAN CLEVE: *The Lamentation over Christ*. Paris, Louvre

203. Joos van Cleve: *Virgin and Child*. Cambridge, Fitzwilliam Museum

204. JOOS VAN CLEVE: *The Holy Family*. New York, Metropolitan Museum of Art

205. PROVOST: *Virgin and Child*. Piacenza, Museo Civico

206. PROVOST: *Virgin and Child with Angels, Prophets and Sibyls*. Leningrad, Hermitage

207. PROVOST: *The Last Judgement*. Bruges, Museum

208. PROVOST: *Death and the Miser*. Bruges, Museum

209. PROVOST: *The Angel appearing to Abraham.* Formerly Paris, Comte Durrieu

210. GOSSAERT: *Resting Apollo* (*'Hermaphrodite'*). Drawing. Venice, Academy

211. GOSSAERT: *Adam and Eve*. Hampton Court Palace.
Reproduced by gracious permission of Her Majesty the Queen

212. Gossaert: *Danae*. Munich, Alte Pinakothek

213. Gossaert: *Neptune and Amphitrite*. Berlin-Dahlem, Staatliche Museen

214. GOSSAERT: *St. Luke painting the Virgin*. Prague, National Gallery

215. GOSSAERT: *St. Luke painting the Virgin*. Vienna, Kunsthistorisches Museum

216. GOSSAERT: *A Man*. Vierhouten, Van Beuningen Collection

217–218. GOSSAERT: *A Donor and his Wife*. Brussels, Museum

219–220. GOSSAERT: *Virgin and Child adored by Jean Carondelet. Paris, Louvre*

221. GOSSAERT: *The Children of Christian II of Denmark.* Hampton Court Palace. Reproduced by gracious permission of Her Majesty the Queen

222. GOSSAERT: *Virgin and Child with Angels*. Centre panel of the Malvagna triptych. Palermo, Museu

223. Gossaert: *The Adoration of the Kings*. London, National Gallery

224. GOSSAERT: *The Agony in the Garden*. Berlin-Dahlem, Staatliche Museen

225. JAN JOEST: *The Virgin and St. John the Evangelist, with the Donor Juan de Fonseca.*
Palencia, Cathedral

226. JAN JOEST: *The Flight into Egypt*. Palencia, Cathedral

227. JAN JOEST: *The Entombment*. Palencia, Cathedral

229. JAN JOEST: *The Baptism of Christ*. Kalkar,
Church of St. Nicholas

228. JAN JOEST: *The Lamentation over Christ*. Cologne,
Wallraf-Richartz Museum

230. MASTER OF FRANKFURT: *The Holy Kindred*. Frankfurt, Staedel Institute

231. MASTER OF FRANKFURT: *The Nativity* (detail). Valenciennes, Museum

232. MASTER OF FRANKFURT: *The Artist and his Wife*. Rome, Baron van der Elst Collection

233. Jan Mostaert: *Joost van Bronckhorst*. Paris, Petit Palais

235. JAN MOSTAERT: *Justina van Wassenaer.* Würzburg,
Martin von Wagner Museum

234. JAN MOSTAERT: *A Man.* Liverpool,
Walker Art Gallery

236. JAN MOSTAERT: *Abraham and Hagar.* Lugano-Castagnola, Schloss Rohoncz Collection, Thyssen Bequest

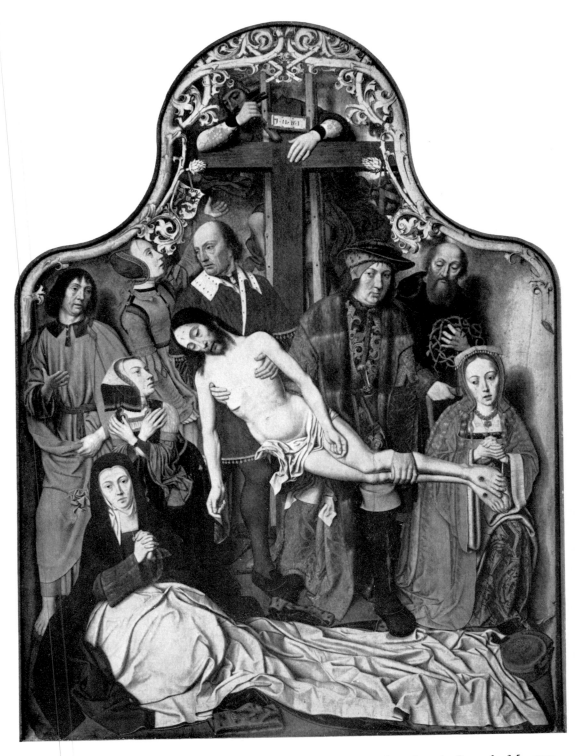

237. JAN MOSTAERT: *The Descent from the Cross*. Centre panel of a triptych. Brussels, Museum

238. JAN MOSTAERT: *The Man of Sorrows*. Verona, Museum

240. JAN MOSTAERT: *The Tree of Jesse*. (Also attributed to

239. JAN MOSTAERT: *The Adoration of the Kings*. Amsterdam,

241. JAN MOSTAERT: *Landscape in the West Indies*. Haarlem, Frans Hals Museum

242. JACOB CORNELISZ. VAN OOSTSAANEN: *Jacob Pijnssen*. Enschede, Rijksmuseum Twenthe

243. Jacob Cornelisz. van Oostsaanen: *Virgin and Child with Angels*. Centre panel of a triptych.
Berlin-Dahlem, Staatliche Museen

244. Jacob Cornelisz. van Oostsaanen: *Noli me tangere*. Cassel, Museum

245. CORNELIS ENGELBRECHTSEN: *St. Constantine and St. Helena*. Munich, Alte Pinakothek

246. LUCAS VAN LEYDEN: *Mohammed and the Monk*. Engraving

247. Lucas van Leyden: *Adam and Eve*. Engraving

248. Lucas van Leyden: *Ecce homo.* Engraving

249. Lucas van Leyden: *Moses striking Water from the Rock*. Boston, Museum of Fine Arts

250. Lucas van Leyden: *The Card Players*. Wilton House, Earl of Pembroke

251. Lucas van Leyden: *The Chess Players*. Berlin-Dahlem, Staatliche Museen

252. Lucas van Leyden: *The Sermon*. Amsterdam, Rijksmuseum

253. LUCAS VAN LEYDEN: *The Worship of the Golden Calf*. Amsterdam, Rijksmuseum

254. Lucas van Leyden: *The Last Judgement.* Leyden, Lakenhal Museum

255. *Angels.* Detail from plate 254

256. *The Damned in Hell*. Detail from plate 254

257–258. *Saints Peter and Paul.* Reverse of the wings of plate 254

259. *Landscape*. Detail from plate 257

260. *Landscape*. Detail from plate 258

261. LUCAS VAN LEYDEN: *Virgin and Child with St. Mary Magdalen and a Donor.*
Munich, Alte Pinakothek

262. LUCAS VAN LEYDEN: *Susanna before the Judge.* Formerly Bremen, Kunsthalle

263. LUCAS VAN LEYDEN: *Self-Portrait*. Brunswick, Herzog Anton Ulrich Museum

264. JAN VAN SCOREL: *The Holy Kindred*. Centre panel of an altarpiece. Obervellach (Carinthia), Chur

265. JAN VAN SCOREL: *The Presentation in the Temple*. Vienna, Kunsthistorisches Museum

266. JAN VAN SCOREL: *Christ's Entry into Jerusalem.* Centre panel of the Lochorst altarpiece. Utrecht, Centraal Museum

267. Jan van Scorel: *The Invention of the Cross*. Centre panel of an altarpiece. Breda, Church

268. *Six Heads*. Detail from plate 267

269. JAN VAN SCOREL: *Twelve Jerusalem Pilgrims*. Haarlem, Frans Hals Museum

270. JAN VAN SCOREL (also attributed to Antonis Mor): *Five Jerusalem Pilgrims*. Utrecht, Centraal Museum

271. JAN VAN SCOREL: *A Schoolboy*. Rotterdam, Museum Boymans-van Beuningen

272. JAN VAN SCOREL: *A Man*. Berlin-Dahlem, Staatliche Museen

273. Jan van Scorel: *A Jerusalem Pilgrim*. Bloomfield Hills (Mich.), Cranbrook Academy of Art

274. JAN VAN SCOREL: *Agatha von Schoonhoven*. Rome, Galleria Doria

276. Maerten van Heemskerck: *Family Group*. Cassel, Museum

277–278. Maerten van Heemskerck: *St. Luke painting the Virgin*. Haarlem, Frans Hals Museum

279–280. Maerten van Heemskerck: *Pieter Bicker and his Wife*. Amsterdam, Rijksmuseum

282. VERMEYEN: *A Man.* Wilton House, Earl of Pembroke

281. VERMEYEN: *Erard de la Marck.* Amsterdam, Rijksmusuem

282. PIETER BRUEGEL: *The Triumph of Death*. Madrid, Prado

284. *The Death Cart.* Detail from plate 283

285. PIETER BRUEGEL: *The Return of the Herd*. Vienna, Kunsthistorisches Museum

286. PIETER BRUEGEL: *The Hunters in the Snow.* Vienna, Kunsthistorisches Museum

287. Pieter Bruegel: *The Peasant Wedding*. Vienna, Kunsthistorisches Museum

288. PIETER BRUEGEL: *The Suicide of Saul*. Detail. Vienna, Kunsthistorisches Museum

289. PIETER BRUEGEL: *The Land of Cockaigne*. Munich, Alte Pinakothek

290. PIETER BRUEGEL: *The Peasant Dance*. Vienna, Kunsthistorisches Museum

291. PIETER BRUEGEL: *The Birdnester*. Vienna, Kunsthistorisches Museum

292. PIETER BRUEGEL: *The Parable of the Blind*. Naples, Museum

293. Pieter Bruegel: *Head of Satan*. Detail from the *Dulle Griet*.
Antwerp, Museum Mayer van den Bergh

# LIST OF PLATES
# INDEX OF PLACES

# ACKNOWLEDGEMENTS

Plates 194, 211 and 221 are reproduced by gracious permission of Her Majesty the Queen.

Plate VI is reproduced by gracious permission of His Serene Highness the Prince of Liechtenstein.

We wish to express our sincere gratitude to the following private owners and museum authorities for permission to reproduce paintings in their collections and for supplying photographs:

The late Mr. D. G. van Beuningen; the late Captain E. G. Spencer Churchill; His Excellency Baron van der Elst; Mme von Pannwitz; the Earl of Pembroke; the late Earl of Radnor; Mrs. Weld Blundell.

Rijksmuseum, Amsterdam; Musée Royal, Antwerp; Museum of Fine Arts, Boston; College van Kerkvoogden, Breda; Herzog Anton Ulrich Museum, Brunswick; Fitwilliam Museum, Cambridge; Museum, Cassel; Art Institute, Chicago; Wallraf-Richartz Museum, Cologne; Institute of Arts, Detroit; Rijksmuseum Twenthe, Enschede; Staedel Institute, Frankfurt; Frans Hals Museum, Haarlem; Lakenhal, Leyden; Walker Art Gallery, Liverpool; National Gallery, London; Castle Rohoncz Collection, Lugano-Castagnola; Prado, Madrid; Alte Pinakothek, Munich; Metropolitan Museum, New York; Museum, Oldenburg; Museum Boymans-Van Beuningen, Rotterdam; Centraal Museum, Utrecht; Kunsthistorisches Museum, Vienna; Art Museum, Worcester, Mass.; and Martin von Wagner Museum, Würzburg.

Further photographs have been supplied by A.C.L., Brussels; De Spaarnestad, Haarlem; Alinari, Florence; Archives Photographiques, Paris; Bulloz, Paris; Giraudon, Paris; and Anderson, Rome.

# LIST OF PLATES

BERNAERT VAN ORLEY (*c.* 1488–1541)
160–161. Ruin of the Children of Job. *Brussels*
162. Charles V. *Budapest*
163. Dr. Georg van Zelle. *Brussels*

QUENTIN MASSYS (1465/6–1530)
164. Virgin and Child. *Brussels*
165. Rest on the Flight into Egypt. *Worcester, Mass.*
166. Entombment. *Antwerp*
167–168. Holy Kindred. *Brussels*
169. Mary Magdalen. *Antwerp*
170. Christ presented to the people. *Madrid*
171. Holy Trinity and Virgin and Child. *Munich*
172. A man. *Frankfurt*
173. A man. *Edinburgh*
174–175. A man and his wife. *Oldenburg*
176. Man with a pink. *Chicago*
177. Money Changer and his wife. *Paris*
178. Erasmus of Rotterdam. *Rome, Galleria Nazionale, Palazzo Corsini*
179. Petrus Aegidius. *Longford Castle, Earl of Radnor*
180. Temptation of St. Anthony. *Madrid*

JOACHIM DE PATENIER (died 1524)
180. Temptation of St. Anthony. *Madrid*
181. Rest on the Flight into Egypt. *Madrid*
182. St. Christopher. *Escorial*
183. Charon crossing the Styx. *Madrid*
184. Baptism of Christ. *Vienna*
185. Flight into Egypt. *Antwerp*

HERRI MET DE BLES
186. Flight into Egypt. *London, Hallsborough Gallery*

CORNELIS MASSYS
(before 1508?–after 1580)
187. St. Jerome in the Wilderness. *Antwerp*
188. The Virgin and St. Joseph arriving in Bethlehem. *Berlin–Dahlem*

MASTER OF THE FEMALE
HALF-LENGTHS
189. Three ladies making music. *Vienna, Harrach Collection*
190. Adoration of the Kings. *Regensburg, Museum*

ADRIAEN YSENBRANDT (died 1551)
191. Seven Sorrows of the Virgin. *Bruges, Notre-Dame*
192. Gold-weigher. *New York*

JOOS VAN CLEVE (died 1540–1)
193. Woman with rosary. *Florence*
194. Henry VIII. *Hampton Court*
195. Eleanor of France. *Vienna*
196. Adoration of the Kings. *Detroit*
197. Death of the Virgin. *Munich*
198. Death of the Virgin (detail). *Cologne*
199. Holy Family. *Vienna*
200. Virgin and Child with Angels. *Lulworth Castle, Col. J. Weld*
201. Rest on the Flight into Egypt. *Brussels*
202. Lamentation over Christ. *Paris*
203. Virgin and Child. *Cambridge*
204. Holy Family. *New York*

JAN PROVOST (*c.*1465?–1529)
205. Virgin and Child. *Piacenza, Museo*
206. Virgin and Child. *Leningrad*
207. Last Judgement. *Bruges*
208. Death and the Miser. *Bruges*
209. Angel appearing to Abraham. *Formerly Paris, Comte Durrieu*

JAN GOSSAERT (died 1532)
210. Resting Apollo ('Hermaphrodite'). Drawing. *Venice, Academy*
211. Adam and Eve. *Hampton Court*
212. Danae. *Munich*
213. Neptune and Amphitrite. *Berlin–Dahlem*
214. St. Luke painting the Virgin. *Prague*
215. St. Luke painting the Virgin. *Vienna*
216. A man. *Vierhouten, Van Beuningen*
217–218. Donor and his wife. *Brussels*
219–220. Virgin and Child adored by Jan Carondelet. *Paris*
221. Three children of Christian II of Denmark. *Hampton Court*
222. Virgin and Child. *Palermo*
223. Adoration of the Kings. *London*
224. Agony in the Garden. *Berlin–Dahlem*

JAN JOEST (died 1519)
225. Virgin and St. John. *Palencia*
226. Flight into Egypt. *Palencia*
227. Entombment. *Palencia*
228. Lamentation. *Cologne*
229. Baptism of Christ. *Kalkar*

### MASTER OF FRANKFURT
230. Holy Kindred. *Frankfurt*
231. Nativity. *Valenciennes*
232. Artist and his wife. *Rome, Baron van der Elst*

### JAN MOSTAERT (*c.* 1472/3–1555/56)
233. Joost van Bronckhorst. *Paris, Petit Palais*
234. A man. *Liverpool*
235. Justina van Wassenaer. *Würzburg*
236. Abraham and Hagar. *Lugano-Castagnola, Castle Rohoncz Collection*
237. Descent from the Cross. *Brussels*
238. Man of Sorrows. *Verona*
239. Adoration of the Kings. *Amsterdam*
240. Tree of Jesse. (Also attributed to Geertgen tot Sint Jans.) *Amsterdam*
241. Landscape in the West Indies. *Haarlem*

### JACOB CORNELISZ. VAN OOSTSAANEN (*c.*1470–1533)
242. Jacob Pijnssen. *Enschede*
243. Virgin and Child. *Berlin–Dahlem*
244. Noli me tangere. *Cassel*

### CORNELIS ENGELBRECHTSZ. (1468?–1533)
245. St. Constantine and St. Helena. *Munich*

### LUCAS VAN LEYDEN (1494–1533)
246. Mohammed and the monk. *Engraving*
247. Adam and Eve. *Engraving*
248. Ecce homo. *Engraving*
249. Moses striking water from the rock. *Boston*
250. Card Players. *Wilton House, Earl of Pembroke*
251. Chess players. *Berlin–Dahlem*
252. Sermon. *Amsterdam*
253. Worship of the golden calf. *Amsterdam*
254–260. Last Judgement. *Leyden, Lakenhal*
261. Virgin and Child with Mary Magdalen. *Munich*
262. Susanna before the judge. *Formerly Bremen, Kunsthalle*
263. Self-portrait. *Brunswick*

### JAN VAN SCOREL (1495–1562)
264. Holy Kindred. *Obervellach*
265. Presentation in the Temple. *Vienna*
266. Christ's Entry into Jerusalem. *Utrecht*
267–268. Invention of the Cross. *Breda*
269. Twelve Jerusalem pilgrims. *Haarlem*
270. Five Jerusalem pilgrims. *Utrecht*
271. Schoolboy. *Rotterdam*
272. A man. *Berlin–Dahlem*
273. Jerusalem pilgrim. *Bloomfield Hills, Mich., Cranbrook Academy*
274. Agatha van Schoonhoven. *Rome, Galleria Doria*
275. Mary Magdalen. *Amsterdam*

### MAERTEN VAN HEEMSKERCK (1498–1574)
276. Family Group. *Cassel*
277–278. St. Luke painting the Virgin. *Haarlem*
279–280. Pieter Bicker and his wife. *Amsterdam*

### JAN VERMEYEN (*c.* 1500–1559)
281. Erard de la Marck. *Amsterdam*
282. A man. *Wilton House, Earl of Pembroke*

### PIETER BRUEGEL (1525/30–1569)
283–284. Triumph of Death. *Madrid*
285. Return of the Herd. *Vienna*
286. Hunters in the Snow. *Vienna*
287. Peasant Wedding. *Vienna*
288. Suicide of Saul. *Vienna*
289. Land of Cockaigne. *Munich*
290. Peasant Dance. *Vienna*
291. Birdnester. *Vienna*
292. Parable of the Blind. *Naples*
293. Dulle Griet (detail). *Antwerp, Museum Mayer van den Bergh*

# COLOUR PLATES

VI. Massys: Portrait of a Canon. *Vaduz, Liechtenstein Collection*
VII. Lucas van Leyden: Adoration of the Kings. *Chicago*
VIII. Lucas van Leyden: Healing of the Blind Man. *Leningrad*
IX. Pieter Bruegel: Children's Games (detail). *Vienna*

# INDEX OF PLACES

AMSTERDAM, Rijksmuseum
Mostaert, 239–40; Lucas, 252, 253; Scorel, 275; Heemskerck, 279–80; Vermeyen, 281

ANTWERP, Musée Royal
Massys, 166, 169; Patenier, 185; Cornelis Massys, 187

ANTWERP, Museum Mayer van den Bergh
Bruegel, 293

BERLIN-DAHLEM, Staatliche Museen
Cornelis Massys, 188; Gossaert, 213, 224; Oostsaanen, 243; Lucas, 251; Scorel, 272

BLOOMFIELD HILLS (Mich.), Cranbrook Academy
Scorel, 273

BOSTON, Museum of Fine Arts
Lucas, 249

BREDA, Church
Scorel, 267–8

BREMEN, Kunsthalle (formerly)
Lucas, 262

BRUGES, Museum
Provost, 207, 208

BRUGES, Notre-Dame
Ysenbrandt, 191

BRUNSWICK, Herzog Anton Ulrich Museum
Lucas, 263

BRUSSELS, Musées Royaux
Orley, 160, 161, 163; Massys, 164, 167, 168; Joos van Cleve, 201; Gossaert, 217–18; Mostaert, 237

BUDAPEST, Museum
Orley, 162

CAMBRIDGE, Fitzwilliam Museum
Joos van Cleve, 203

CASSEL, Museum
Oostsaanen, 244; Heemskerck, 276

CHICAGO, Art Institute
Lucas, VII; Massys, 176

COLOGNE, Wallraf-Richartz Museum
Joos van Cleve, 198; Joest, 228

DETROIT, Institute of Arts
Joos van Cleve, 196

EDINBURGH, National Gallery of Scotland
Goes, 100 (on loan from Palace of Holyroodhouse); Massys, 173

ENSCHEDE, Rijksmuseum Twenthe
Oostsaanen, 242

ESCORIAL
Patenier, 182

FLORENCE, Uffizi
Joos van Cleve, 193

FRANKFURT, Staedel Institute
Massys, 172; Master of Frankfurt, 230

HAARLEM, Frans Hals Museum
Mostaert, 241; Scorel, 269; Heemskerck, 277–8

HAMPTON COURT, Palace
Joos van Cleve, 194; Gossaert, 211, 221

KALKAR, St. Nicholas
Joest, 229

LENINGRAD, Hermitage
Lucas, VIII; Provost, 206

LEYDEN, Lakenhal
Lucas, 254–60

LIVERPOOL, Walker Art Gallery
Mostaert, 234

LONDON, Hallsborough Gallery
Herri met de Bles, 186

LONDON, National Gallery
Gossaert, 223

LONGFORD CASTLE, Earl of Radnor
Massys, 179

LUGANO, Castle Rohoncz Collection
Mostaert, 236

LULWORTH MANOR, Col. J. Weld
Collection
Joos van Cleeve, 200

MADRID, Prado
Massys, 170, 180; Patenier, 181, 183;
Bruegel, 283–4

MUNICH, Alte Pinakothek
Massys, 171; Joos van Cleve, 197;
Gossaert, 212; Engelbrechtsz., 245; Lucas,
261; Bruegel, 289

NAPLES, Museum
Bruegel, 292

NEW YORK, Metropolitan Museum
Ysenbrandt, 192; Joos van Cleve, 204

OBERVELLACH, Church
Scorel, 264

OLDENBURG, Museum
Massys, 174–5

PALENCIA, Cathedral
Joest, 225–7

PALERMO, Museum
Gossaert, 222

PARIS, Louvre
Massys, 177; Joos van Cleve, 202;
Gossaert, 219–20

PARIS, Petit Palais
Mostaert, 233

PARIS, Comte Durrieu (formerly)
Provost, 209

PIACENZA, Museo Civico
Provost, 205

PRAGUE, National Gallery
Gossaert, 214

REGENSBURG, Museum
Master of the Female Half-Lengths, 190

ROME, Galleria Nazionale, Palazzo
Corsini
Massys, 178; Scorel, 271

ROME, Galleria Doria
Scorel, 274

ROME, Baron van der Elst
Collection
Master of Frankfurt, 232

UTRECHT, Centraal Museum
Scorel, 266, 270

VADUZ, Liechtenstein Collection
Massys, VI

VALENCIENNES, Museum
Master of Frankfurt, 231

VENICE, Academy
Gossaert, 210

VERONA, Museum
Mostaert, 238

VIENNA, Kunsthistorisches Museum
Patenier, 184; Joos van Cleve, 195, 199;
Gossaert, 215; Scorel, 265; Bruegel, IX,
285–8 290–1

VIENNA, Harrach Collection
Master of the Female Half-Lengths, 189

VIERHOUTEN, Van Beuningen
Collection
Gossaert, 216

WILTON HOUSE, Earl of Pembroke
Lucas, 250; Vermeyen, 282

WORCESTER, Mass., Art Museum
Massys, 165

WÜRZBURG, Martin von Wagner
Museum
Mostaert, 235